The Fur-Bearing Trout...

and Other True Tales of Canadian Life

ISBN: 978-0-9921356-5-2

Book and cover design: Heather Greenwood
Editor: Cecilia Buy
Printed in Canada by Sportswood Printing, Straffordville, Ontario

The authors gratefully acknowledge the financial support of the London Arts Council and City of London

INTRODUCTION

The late Jack Layton once said "Canada is a great country, one of the hopes of the world." In these pages you'll read stories of hope, not just by those of us born here but by others who came to this country from elsewhere. You'll also read accounts of childhood memories from different parts of the country, how Canadians feel when they're outside Canada, what it's like to engage with nature in this vast land, and chronicles of iconic touchstones that make our country unique.

We are a group of professional writers who either live or have lived in London, Ontario at some point in our careers and who are current or former members of the Professional Writers Association of Canada. But these stories are not just about our corner of the world in southwestern Ontario. They cover the breadth of the nation, and we hope these true tales of Canadian life will resonate with readers everywhere. Within this book, you will encounter a famous dead elephant, a national hero, possibly Canada's worst ever hockey team, train travellers, a persistent bear, beautiful sunsets and northern lights. All of them hold some kind of truth that can help us better understand this country – even one about a fur-bearing trout. Enjoy.

COMING FROM AWAY

Coming to Canada...9
This Place I Call Home...14
Home Child...20
Double Dead, But Not Forgotten..........................25
I Am Canadian...40

GROWING UP CANADIAN

Five Assists 47
Niagara Falls - Victoria Day
    A Canadian Heritage Lesson 53
How the Game Began..58
Centennial Year...62
Home Again 67

TRAVELS NEAR AND FAR

A Hero in Any Language......................................75
The Fur-Bearing Trout 81
Hooked on Travel by Rail...................................86
Playing in the Shadow of Vimy..........................94
Giant Things and Other Scraps of Trivia.............99

THE GREAT OUTDOORS

Day Six 107
A True Canadian Sunset....................................119
Wild Side 123
Celebration of Light...131
Planting Hope...134

OTHER TRUE TALES

Time Travel...145
Legacy of the Worn Out Shoes
    A Canadian ParticipACTION Story...................151
The Secret That Won the War 154
Hans Across the Water 163
My Stratford Debut 168

ABOUT THE AUTHORS 172

Coming From Away

COMING TO CANADA

BY PATRICIA PATERSON

Pier 21 in the port city of Halifax was an ocean-liner terminal and immigration depot from 1928 until 1971. It is often compared to the American immigration gateway, Ellis Island. In 1997 it was designated as a National Interpretive Centre and Historic Site. The Canadian Museum of Immigration now hosts a database and interpretive centre, which documents immigration to Canada through this port of entry.

It is estimated that over one million immigrants passed through Pier 21. My family was among those who immigrated in 1956: a time of unprecedented post-war economic migration from Britain, Italy, Germany, the Netherlands and other European countries. Newcomers to Canada, then as now, came with the hope of a better future for themselves and their children.

I remember the day my father announced that we were going to Canada. It was not unusual for my father, a Marine Engineer used to seafaring adventures, to cause some commotion or another on his shore leave. However, this one surpassed them all. The news was received with a long, heart-wrenching wail from my mother, "Canada! We can't just go sailing away to Canada!"

There were older family members still living in the west coast Scottish town to consider. Many of the younger ones had already left: an uncle to the copper mines in Rhodesia (Zimbabwe); an aunt to the United States with her American husband; and another aunt to England. We were among the few who still remained. My father decided to ease the transition by preceding us by a year to get established. Eventually, it would be our turn to sail westward.

In June of 1956 we boarded the SS Lismoria at the port of Greenock. We watched the gangplank hoisted and the moorings released. Our ship pulled away from the pier. On the wharf below, the old aunties stood quietly weeping and waving handkerchiefs. So many Scots left from Greenock to Canada that there is a promontory, overlooking the Firth of Clyde, named Canada Hill. Families used to climb up Canada Hill to catch the last glimpse of departing loved ones as their ships headed out to sea.

Crossing the Atlantic by ship took about a week, unlike the overnight flights of today. A week at sea gave you time to think about what the future might bring. This trans-Atlantic crossing was not my first time at sea. During summer vacations, I sailed with my father on the Lady Anstruther, a coastal freighter that carried dynamite to the coal mines in Wales. Coastal waters of the North and the Irish Seas could be pretty rough. However, this was my first big sea adventure. I was in my element and never once missed a meal due to seasickness. The resiliency of youth is not to be underestimated.

On June 7, 1956, my mother and I walked down the gangplank and into the port terminal of Pier 21. I remember a two-storey shed of steel trusses with brick walls and through that an annex containing immigration and custom offices. As a minor child, I was on my mother's passport. The immigration officer stamped the passport and then looked up with a smile. "Welcome to Canada."

We returned to the ship to continue our voyage up the St. Lawrence River, as we were disembarking at the port of Montreal. The St. Lawrence Seaway boasts the largest estuary in the world, running some 3,056 kilometres to Quebec City. It provides a magnificent first impression of Canada. As we sailed northwest, the sunset of a soft June evening was unforgettable. The flower-scented summer breezes so different from the bracing winds of Scotland. It was my first day in Canada as a landed immigrant.

As we neared Quebec City, we could see Chateau

Frontenac off the starboard side of the ship. Built in 1893 as part of the Canadian Pacific Railway series of hotels, the Chateau gave an impression of tradition and grandeur reminiscent of the stately castles of Scotland. It was comforting to know that the Scots had been established in Canada for centuries. I later learned that five days following the death of General James Wolfe during the battle of the Plains of Abraham in 1759, it was Brigadier-General James Murray who accepted the capitulation of the French forces. Murray, fluently bilingual, had led the Fraser's Highland regiment, and later became the first British Governor of Quebec. Many of the Highlanders settled in this area. If you tour old Quebec City you will see Celtic designs and Gaelic inscriptions on the doorways and lintels of old homes.

My father met us in Montreal. He was driving an old Ford Customline with a beige body and a chocolate brown roof. All our worldly possessions were jammed into that old car and off we went to Toronto. Our first apartment was a three-storey walk-up between Bloor and College Streets. Culture shock was a daily occurrence and often a source of humour. I went through my first winter in Canada with a British cloth coat, kilt, and leather brogues. We soon learned about snowsuits! I got my first one the next winter at Honest Ed's Warehouse, a vile mustard yellow thing.

Life has been good in Canada. It is said that the remarkable advance of the early Scottish settlers was attributed to their famous work ethic. My family followed that time-honoured formula. I became a schoolteacher and raised two Canadian sons. There are now four grandchildren who light up my life. I have travelled through most of Canada, with the exception of the Yukon and Nunavut. However, that first impression of a setting sun over the St. Lawrence River on a June evening has been the most lasting. I returned to

Pier 21 a few years ago, to find the records of our immigration. More than 60 years since I first went through the Port of Halifax, my records were still there.

Photo courtesy of Patricia Paterson
The author, just prior to leaving Scotland, with her great-uncle, Alasdair Macrae

THIS PLACE I CALL HOME

BY SUZANNE BOLES

B orn in Canada with one foot on American soil, I have always felt a kinship to both countries but chose Canada as my home. It's the home of my parents and grandparents, but I'm the only one of my immediate family who decided to make this their forever-after country.

My father and mother met in London, Ontario where I live today. Dad was attending The (then) University of Western Ontario medical school and Mom was a nursing student. They had both been born and raised in Windsor, Ontario, on the border of Detroit, Michigan where you could stand by the river's edge on either side and see the other country.

It was actually surprising that my parents never met in Windsor, which was a fairly small city during WWII, with an even smaller Jewish community in the post-war era. Both of their parents were active Jewish community members, but it wasn't until they were both in London that they finally met.

Mom said she wasn't impressed with Dad at their

first meeting, but obviously that changed because, not long after, they started dating. Their first encounter was at a dance and, like Cinderella with a modern twist, Mom's earring fell off and landed in the cuff of his pants (a style all the rage in the 1950s). Dad later located Mom's family and told my grandmother he had Mom's earring, and asked if she could relay the message so he could return it. That eventually led to a marriage that lasted over five decades.

In their first years of marital bliss and financial struggle, Mom worked as a nurse while Dad was completing his medical residency. Not long after, they learned they were expecting me. Mom always said I was a "joyful surprise," which, loosely translated, meant unexpected. They wanted kids, it just happened earlier than planned. Mom said she wanted two children, two years apart. Two years later my sister obliged.

Dad was a radiologist. He wanted to use his expertise to enter the brave new world of cancer research and treatment, in the hope of finding a cure in his lifetime. He saw his opportunity in the U.S., so the young couple scrimped and saved (with some help from their parents who didn't have a lot of money either) and built their dream house in Farmington, Michigan, qualifying for the $25,000 mortgage. We moved there when I was five.

Mom chose to stay at home to raise us. She was a wonderful homemaker and cook. She had many friends and enjoyed social outings, volunteering and being a member of the women's Jewish Hadassah.

My parents couldn't afford to completely furnish our house for several years, so the living and dining room parquet floors were a place for my sister and me to practice gymnastics. Despite early financial strains they faced, we were never wanting for food, clothing, love or anything else. But I never really felt like I fit in at home or in my hometown.

We were the only ones in our neighbourhood who were Jewish. Bringing matzah for lunch at school during Passover created two camps among my classmates – those who marveled at it and those who scoffed.

Everything in the U.S. felt like it was moving faster than the speed of light, as the Americans raced against the Russians to put the first man in space (the Russians won) and to plant their flag on the moon (the Americans won).

I struggled with math and science – ironic since my parents were both in the medical field – but excelled in my love of reading and writing.

My most cherished memories are of crossing the border to my native Canada. Each time I visited Canada as a youngster I could feel a palpable difference between the north and south border countries. There was a quieter, easier pace in the northern country. People were friendly and it always felt like home.

We often visited our grandparents, (Dad's parents), who lived in Windsor with Dad's brother, Uncle Lew. Lew and Dad were 21 years apart, so our uncle was more like an older cousin to us. The home they lived in was built by our grandfather and Dad. There was the girl next door – Margot – who was about my age. I loved hanging out with her eating raspberries and sour rhubarb directly from my grandmother's garden.

Our cousins and their parents lived in St. Thomas, Ontario. I loved visiting the small town where my uncle owned a shoe store on the main drag – so different from the big shopping plazas sprouting up all over suburban Detroit. When we were younger, my uncle would meticulously fit my sister and me for shoes before the start of the school year. We'd go to Springbank Park and Storybook Gardens in London, Ontario, sliding down inside a whale depicting the story of Jonah, and squealing with laughter. We loved the zoo animals and enjoyed an ice cream cone on a hot summer's day.

As teenagers my sister and I would visit my grand-parents, who had moved to Toronto after Uncle Lew had a tragic accident and needed care and rehabilitation to adjust to his life as a quadriplegic. We adored taking the train to the sparkling, big city with its skyscrapers, old fashioned streetcars, modern subways and little crime; far different from Detroit where a venture into the city meant locking your car doors and being hypervigilant against possible peril.

My sister and I would push Lew in his wheelchair at the Canadian National Exhibition (CNE) grounds and Ontario Place – just a short walk from my grandparents' apartment. Looking back, I can hardly believe he trusted two skinny teenagers who held tightly to his wheelchair as we went down those steep, narrow ramps, barely able to hang on. We shared cigarettes and laughter. We thought we were VIPs, getting into venues for free – Canadians were wonderful in recognizing that people with disabilities should be given caring treatment, and many people would stop and help us, insisting on opening doors.

I knew I really wanted to live in this very different country, and the big shining city beckoned me home. So when it came time to think about university – in our family it wasn't a question of if, but when – I applied and was accepted to York University in Toronto. Though the Canadian dollar was worth more than the U.S. buck then, I would only need three years for a Bachelor of Arts degree, as opposed to four in the U.S., and Canadian universities accepted American students for equal to Canadian student tuition, another bonus.

I crossed the border in 1973 and it didn't take me long to realize that this is where I belonged. Aside from initial razzing from fellow students about the Vietnam War, I was accepted by my peers. I loved going to downtown Toronto, checking out the vinyl at Sam the Record Man and visiting my grandmother, who worked in the makeup department at Woolworth's where we'd eat at the famous lunch counter on her break. Sometimes she'd slip me an overstock of the newest shade of lipstick.

I married someone I met at York and stayed in Canada after graduation. I divorced, married my husband Bob, and eventually we settled in London, where my daughter and two stepchildren also got to enjoy visiting Storybook Gardens and sliding into the whale's belly.

I've lived in London for almost 30 years now. Bob passed away in 2013 and I'm not sure London will remain my home, but I do know that this side of the border is where I plan to stay. I love visiting my sister, who lives in Virginia, but I'm always glad to drive over the border at Sarnia or Windsor and to feel the Canadian spirit re-enter me in this place I call home.

HOME CHILD

BY NANCY LOUCKS-MCSLOY

O n April 6, 1835 my great-great grandmother, nine-year old Laney Israel, would embark on a journey halfway around the world and settle in a new country, working as a housemaid, growing up, marrying and raising a family.

She was an orphan, a waif, a stray living in an orphanage in Chiswick, England. The orphanage was part of the Children's Friend Society with a goal of teaching the children domestic and farm duties. The girls could work as housemaids for the elite and the boys on farms. The reason behind this idea was to stop vagrancy. By the early 1830s people of the Children's Friend Society found that this was not feasible. As a result some of the children were sent to Cape of Good Hope and some were sent to a new frontier, Upper Canada.

Laney was sitting in her classroom that fateful day when a man entered the school and said, "Who's for the new country?" Laney and a friend quickly put up their hands and shouted "We are!" They were whisked out of the classroom with just the clothes on their backs – nothing else – and soon boarded the tall ship *Toronto* for the long trek to Montreal.

The trip was treacherous to say the least. The ship's master, Collinson, and a handful of passengers spent nearly 40 days on the ship that was filled with general cargo. In later years Laney would tell her family of the rough seas, the sickness, the deaths, the morbidity of people being thrown overboard and the horrible, filthy conditions on the *Toronto*. Finally on May 11, 1835, the ship docked in Montreal.

Here was a nine-year-old girl in a totally new country. At that time the population of Upper Canada was approximately 350,000. It was a new land with few people. Other than the First Nations and Inuit peoples, everyone was new to the country. Laney's trip was not complete though. Very soon she was boarding a St. Lawrence Steamboat Company vessel and travelling to her new home near Kingston. Once in Kingston she was placed in the home of a Mr. John B. Merchant and became a housemaid for the family.

The work would have been hard for a nine-year-old, but she had no other option. Laney spent her years growing into adulthood in the Kingston area and on September 28, 1847, she married Edward Castle Loucks, a wagon maker from Napanee and a United Empire Loyalist descendant. They farmed in the area until 1863, when they moved first to

Durham and then to their homestead in Amabel Township, close to Sauble Beach. The hard work did not stop when Laney left her job as a housemaid. She lived on a farm from the time she was married until her death in 1908. Laney and Edward raised eight children during very difficult times. As was often the case in the 1800s, they lost several children at birth. The infants are buried in a small cemetery on the family homestead.

The distance from Kingston to Durham is nearly 300 miles. Once again Laney embarked on another journey, this time with her husband and family in a Conestoga wagon. In 1863 the trip would have taken many days over rough roads. The next trek from Durham to Sauble Beach, which is approximately 50 miles, would have been another long journey, once again over rough roads and trails.

As I think about this, and about what that little girl must have endured, I cannot begin to imagine what she would have been feeling. She had no idea as to what her future would hold. She was on her own in absolutely horrendous conditions on a ship, and then given away as child labour. When I walk my nine-year-old granddaughter to her school bus stop, I often think about the fact that she is indeed the same age as her great, great, great-grandmother had been when she ventured out into a new frontier by herself. My granddaughter is not allowed to leave the street. Laney left her homeland!

My perception of Laney is that of being a very brave, free-spirited child. Perhaps she was a bit bizarre or spontaneous, acting on a whim. There is a possibility that she felt that anything would be better than life in an orphanage. Whatever the case may be, she was one of many who paved the way for future generations. I speak of Laney with great pride, even though I never met her.

Laney was one of the earlier children to be brought to Canada, but by 1869 larger numbers of Home Children were being sent to the British colonies, particularly Canada, Australia and New Zealand, mainly to farming families — more than 100,000 in total, the largest migration of children in the history of the world. They were a large, unpaid labour force for many of Canada's early settlers.

The Government of Canada declared 2010 to be the Year of the British Home Child, and in September of that year Canada Post released a commemorative stamp. In 2011 the Government of Ontario proclaimed September 28 as British Home Child Day to recognize and honour the contributions of the British Home Children who established roots in Ontario.

As you head east on Sauble Beach's Main Street, you will come across Zion Amabel Cemetery. There you will see the tall white tombstone which marks Laney's final resting place. Where would we be today if it were not for Laney and the many others who braved all odds and set out on an incredible journey, helping to make Canada the great country that we love?

DOUBLE DEAD, BUT NOT FORGOTTEN

BY MARY ANN COLIHAN

My husband worked hard to show me the local sights he thought might make me feel settled in London when I moved here in 1988. So on our first outing he went big — really big.

Jumbo in fact. He found my college mascot in St. Thomas.

There, up on a hill, butt-end facing out to the highway, is the roadside attraction of my dreams. Jumbo the elephant! Phineas Taylor Barnum's stuffed contribution to Tufts University died here in 1885 – struck dead by a Grand Trunk freight train after an evening circus performance. A century later, the City of St. Thomas erected a cement Jumbo replica to honour a truly sad train wreck. Once again, I was in the orbit of P.T. Barnum, former mayor of Bridgeport, Connecticut, my birthplace, and a founding trustee of Tufts. The reach of this long-dead showman knew no bounds – certainly not the 49th parallel.

Photo courtesy of the Tufts Digital Library

Jumbo is famous in St. Thomas, Ontario where he was killed by a train in 1885. He is also the mascot of Tufts University – seen here with a bevy of co-eds. As a taxidermy specimen, he met his second demise in a 1975 campus fire. Jumbo with Joan Franceschini Whittaker (far right) and three other unidentified students. 1933

How did Jumbo become a sensation? Why does the English lexicon feature the word jumbo so prominently: jumbo jets, the Jumbo Tron, hockey Shark and St. Thomas native son Jumbo Joe Thornton, the list stretches to include all things large – like the pants waist of those who eat too many jumbo-sized hot dogs with pop.

Jumbo's story starts in Africa in 1859, somewhere near what is now Sudan. Jumbo was snatched by traders when he was barely weaned. Some accounts say he saw his mother brutally murdered. He was brought to Paris and sold to the Jardin des Plantes. In 1865, he and a smaller elephant named Lucy were sent to England's London Zoological Society in exchange for a rhinoceros. Jumbo arrived so half-starved, rat-bitten and sick that his new trainer, Matthew Scott of the London Zoo, thought he had leprosy. Scott nursed him back to health, in his words "with the care and affection of a mother." The two became inseparable. In time, Jumbo developed an enormous appetite and snacked endlessly upon the buns tossed his way with abandon. He was eventually described as the "largest land animal ever in captivity" and grew to over six tons in weight and 11 feet in height.

Jumbo was sweet-natured for a male elephant. Children fell under his charm as they swayed on his massive back. He gave rides to hundreds of thousands of children during his 17 years at the London Zoo, including a young Winston Churchill, U.S. President Teddy Roosevelt, and the royal offspring of Queen Victoria.

He was England's national pet, lumbering along the bucolic pathways of Regent's Park. Harper's Weekly Magazine said he was "as gentle with children as the best trained poodle dog, taking the proffered biscuit or lump of sugar with an almost incredible delicacy of touch. … The most nervous child, having once overcome his alarm, never hesitated to hand a morsel to his waving trunk a second time."

However, the London Zoo had been secretly trying to find a new home for Jumbo, fearful that he would soon fall victim to musth, the periodic inflammation of the male elephant's temporal glands. This occurs during their years of peak sexuality and causes arousal in elephants. They can sometimes become physically aggressive in the company of female elephants – a jumbo problem for a captive pachyderm in Victorian England. Most out-of-control elephant behaviour occurs during musth, and given Jumbo's age, sex and size, the Zoo reasoned there could be fatalities if he went on a rampage.

Enter P.T. Barnum – Connecticut politician, big thinker and the greatest entertainment promoter of the nineteenth century. He coveted Jumbo and knew precisely how to capitalize on his outsize talents. Much to Barnum's surprise, his offer of $10,000 was accepted. Almost immediately, to intensify publicity, Barnum started to leak to the press that the British people were being swindled. Queen Victoria, the Prince of Wales, and editors and up and down Fleet Street expressed dismay that the Empire's prized specimen was being exported to their upstart former colony across the pond. Zoo attendance soared.

Despite legal attempts to invalidate Jumbo's sale, he arrived by ship in New York on Easter Sunday, 1882, where excitement, called Jumbomania, had reached a fever pitch. He was paraded up Broadway straight into Madison Square Garden and the hearts of an adoring public. There was never any question that Matthew Scott could be separated from Jumbo. If he took a day off at the Zoo, Jumbo went berserk. Scott shared Jumbo's cabin on the ocean voyage and kept him sedated with beer and whiskey.

It helps to understand Barnum if you grew up, as I did, in Fairfield, Connecticut – next door to Bridgeport, the epicentre of the Barnum brand. His name is on everything. The Ringling Brothers Barnum and Bailey circus, the Barnum Festival of music with a parade that featured a Ringmaster, and competitions to find the next Jenny Lind, a virtuoso opera singer he discovered and promoted as the "Swedish Nightingale," and the cutest children to crown as Tom Thumb and Lavinia Warren, the two midgets who married each other, and toured with Barnum for years.

The Barnum Museum in Bridgeport houses exhibits from some of his old freak shows. As a young child, I had recurrent nightmares from having seen the "Fejee Mermaid," which was the top half of a monkey sewn on to the bottom of a fish. I recall the exhibit was near the entrance and it usually made me want to flee. I thought Barnum had fished the "mermaid" out of Long Island Sound where I swam.

Barnum made his reputation as the owner of the Manhattan-based American Museum, a mish-mash of historical artifacts and animal and aquatic curiosities. Barnum had two key marketing strategies: use "scientific experts" to explain oddities, and bait the popular press with outlandish stories. He promoted giants, dwarves and midgets, bearded ladies, heavily tattooed men, Siamese twins, and performers like the "female white Moor" and the "Hindu serpent sorceress with a necklace of snakes."

He launched P.T. Barnum's Grand Traveling Museum, Menagerie, Caravan, and Circus in 1871 and called it "The Greatest Show on Earth." In 1881, he partnered with James Bailey to add a three-ring circus under the big tent. Barnum showed the world how to make money from promotional materials and souvenirs. As Jumbo's popularity grew, Barnum took every opportunity to use the word "jumbo" as a synonym for all things "large."

The Barnum and Bailey Circus was a finely tuned touring machine: the Big Tent went up and down, thousands of animals and people were fed, trains were loaded and unloaded, month after summer month. Canada was included on many Barnum and Bailey tours of the 1880s – from the Maritimes through Quebec and Ontario. After more than a hundred stops and 8,000 miles, the circus train pulled into the town of St. Thomas, Ontario in the early hours of September 15, 1885, and rolled to a stop in the Grand Trunk Railroad yards.

Two elephants closed the show that night: tiny Tom Thumb and the mighty Jumbo. Matthew Scott led the elephants back along the main track to Jumbo's circus car as the Grand Trunk's Special Freight Number 151 was nearing the rail yard. Number 151 was not scheduled to stop in St. Thomas and it picked up speed on a downgrade as it approached the yard. As the train's engineer William Burnip scanned the track ahead, he spotted a hulking silhouette over the rails. Too late, he saw he was heading straight at not only one elephant, but two.

Frantic, he tried to reverse, and blew the whistle for the brakeman who had to manually turn the great hand wheels at the end of each boxcar to stop the train. With a horrific screech of metal on metal, the train wheels locked and shot glowing sparks high. Burnip and his fireman had no choice but to leap from the cab at the last instant, to save themselves.

Scott heard the emergency brakes and realized the train approaching in the darkness was on their track. The local flagman sprinted towards it, waving his lantern desperately. Scott got Jumbo to run forward but he was hemmed in on one side by circus cars and would not go down the steep embankment on the other side, to safety. Scott knew they could not outrun the train. First poor Tom Thumb was caught by the train's cowcatcher and spun down the hill, his leg broken.

Jumbo ran past a break in the circus cars but couldn't stop his forward momentum. The locomotive slammed into his backside. Jumbo went to his knees, and the train skidded off the rails with such force that it shoved him violently under the wheel-carriage of a circus car and crushed his massive skull; one tusk was driven back into his brain.

Here is Edgar Flach's eyewitness account of Jumbo's final moments: "The animal… reached out his long trunk, wrapped it around the trainer and then drew him down to where that majestic head lay blood-stained in the cinders. Scotty cried like a baby. Five minutes later, they lifted him from the lifeless body… That night Scotty lay down beside the body of his friend. At last exhausted from the strain, he fell asleep."

As the crowd grew, souvenir hunters armed with knives and scissors attacked, including one opportunist who took a large slice from Jumbo's ear. When Scott discovered the mutilation, he was apoplectic. The St. Thomas police arrived in the morning and posted a guard to protect the corpse.

Barnum, in his wisdom, had already arranged to have Jumbo's hide and skeleton mounted in the event of some mishap. Henry Ward's Natural Science Establishment, a museum-quality taxidermy firm in Rochester, New York, was contracted for this work.

By the time Ward got to St. Thomas, Jumbo had lain dead for two days. Ward carefully measured every dimension of Jumbo's body. Into the evening, several local butchers dissected the rotting corpse. A man named Peters had the dirty job of cleaning out Jumbo's stomach and found a bobby's whistle, a slew of keys, several rivets and a "hatful" of English pennies – no doubt souvenirs of Jumbo's time at the London Zoo.

Barnum told Ward to jumbo-size the corpse. "By all means… let him show like a mountain!" The sections of the 1,538-pound hide were put in baths of salt water and alum and shipped to Rochester in a wooden tank. To prepare Jumbo for his post-mortem circus tour, his skin was cured, scraped, and treated with arsenic to eliminate the danger of decay. A wooden mould was built to Jumbo's corpse measurements. Then his skin was stretched over the mold and fastened down with 44,000 countersunk copper nails. His mangled tusks were replaced with genuine ivory substitutes.

Jumbo's 2,400-pound skeleton was cleaned and his

shattered skull was painstakingly rebuilt with moulds and papier-mâché. When Ward and his talented team finished in March of 1886, the two Jumbos — skeleton and carcass — were delivered back to The Greatest Show on Earth.

Barnum mounted a funeral tour extravaganza. He imported Alice from the London Zoo as Jumbo's "weeping widow." The other circus elephants were trained to wipe their eyes with sheets. For the next two seasons Jumbo's skin and bones were paraded, solemnly, followed by Alice and her herd. All the elephants held black-trimmed sheets in their trunks and wiped their eyes. It was a tour-de-force, or farce. But then, on November 24, 1887, the show's winter quarters in Bridgeport burned to the ground in a horrible conflagration. Alice perished in the flames. Jumbo's remains were saved.

Barnum then bequeathed Jumbo a permanent home at Tufts where he was a founding trustee. With $50,000, he built the Barnum Museum of Natural History on campus in 1884. Jumbo's skeleton was donated to the American Museum of Natural History in New York.

Jumbo became an immediate sensation on campus and was adopted as the college mascot. Athletes and coaches revered his strength and bravery. Songs and poems were written to Jumbo and countless traditions began. It was said that if you dropped a coin in Jumbo's trunk you could get an "A" on exams. Others tugged on his tail for good luck.

I saw Jumbo only once on campus, with my mother and sister in the fall of 1974. We were surprised that Barnum's animal kingdom extended to Massachusetts. I don't remember putting a coin in Jumbo's trunk to gain admission but do recall thinking that he was a cool mascot. Go Jumbos!

When I was accepted at Tufts in 1975, I made a final trip to campus to be sure about my choice. I got off the bus that cool April day to an appalling smell. Sometime after midnight, faulty wiring ignited a fire that consumed the Museum and Barnum's circus posters, letters, his marble bust and desk. Jumbo's hide was incinerated in the blaze. An old elephant carcass pickled in formaldehyde and arsenic leaves a visceral chemical odour that feels sticky in your mouth. Jumbo was now truly Double Dead.

A quick thinking secretary in the athletic department sent a janitor to gather up some of Jumbo's ashes in an empty peanut butter jar. Jumbo lives on in spirit, and since 1975 athletes have rubbed the 14-ounce Peter Pan Crunchy Peanut Butter jar for good luck. I personally have seen the jar sitting on a shelf in Cousens gym, but never rubbed it.

Two years later, in 1977, a plaque with the history of Jumbo's death was unveiled in St. Thomas. By then the community, once known as Railway City, had lost all passenger rail and freight service. A Jumbo Centennial Committee was formed to create a monument to the most famous railway accident in Canadian history. New Brunswick artist Winston Bronnum was selected to sculpt Jumbo's likeness and on June 28, 1985 Ruby Copeman, age 106, unveiled Jumbo's statue. She was the last St. Thomas resident to have witnessed Jumbo either dead or alive.

When I met Jumbo as a roadside attraction, I hardly knew him. Since then, I have visited archives and had conversations with historians. A bookstore in Bethel, Connecticut, within sight of Barnum's home, is my favourite stop for chats about Barnum and out-of-print books about Jumbo. And without thinking, I started to acquire elephant stuff: red gingham Christmas ornaments shaped like elephants, mini-teaspoons with elephants on the handle that I gave to my Jumbo girlfriends for our 25th anniversary, Mammut t-shirts with a logo of a jumbo Mammoth, a wooden curtain rod capped with elephant's heads – that sort of thing. My husband's sabbatical in France immersed us in Babar the elephant. My three boys read Babar books en français, ate off Babar plates and dreamt sweet dreams under Babar posters.

As I learn more about elephants in the wild, my wish is that they could live and socialize safely with their families. Statistics are grim: a recent census estimates there are 352,271 African elephants and 74 are killed each day for their ivory, which is sold as "medicine" or carved into jewelry and trinkets. And they don't thrive in cold climates. The Edmonton Valley Zoo is lovely, but Lucy still lives there in a squat concrete house I found too small for her jumbo-ness. But, like those children at the London Zoo, I jump at the chance to ride on an elephant's back – first in India and then with my kids at the African Lion Safari. Maybe that isn't good for them either. So as my relationship with these beautiful beasts evolves, my mascot will be my muse.

I've met Canadians who share my interest in Jumbo's history. The most avid fan is Steve Peters, the former MPP, cabinet minister, speaker of the house and Mayor of St. Thomas. He's a savvy collector of Jumbo material and in 2004, after graduating from Western's journalism school, I did a Rogers TV documentary on his collection. We spoke of his Tufts campus visit when he met with Rocky Carzo, Tufts' athletic director, who, in a gesture of cross-border goodwill, gave him some of Jumbo's ashes to take back to Canada.

Jumbo is home here. In 2006, when I managed the revival of the Horton Farmer's Market in St. Thomas, we held a Jumbo Day with all kinds of jumbo-themed products and a vendor dressed up as a pachyderm. When Mike Baker at the Elgin County Museum mounted a truly wonderful

Jumbo show in 2014, Steve Peters lent some of his best pieces. These include a rare cross-section of Jumbo's tusk that names him the "King of Elephants" and a sterling silver bowl that Barnum presented to the London Zoo after he bought Jumbo for his circus. No doubt he viewed this purchase as the deal of a lifetime.

Since 1885, the oversized narrative arc of Jumbo's life – from abandoned African orphan to England's pet to North America's first celebrity superstar endorser – has led to countless promotions. Companies that have profited from Jumbo's name include a brand of ginger beer, shoe polish, peanut butter and turpentine. His visage adorned cigar boxes from Honsinger, one of three St. Thomas cigar makers.

They say elephants never forget but it is Jumbo who is unforgotten.

My favourite Jumbo products include smoothies from Jumbo Juice in Bayfield and videos from my local Jumbo Video store, also an endangered species. The Railway City Brewing Company, a craft brewery in St. Thomas, have products including their Dead Elephant Ale with the tagline "A Jumbo legend with an Unforgettable Taste!" They also brew a Double Dead Elephant IPA to honour Jumbo's second passing at Tufts when his 90-year-old carcass went up in smoke. Their beers capture both Jumbo's historical significance to St. Thomas and one of my old school's legendary moments.

My husband could not have found a better spot to bind me to Canada.

Photo of Jumbo's statue in St. Thomas courtesy of Gail McNaughton; Doodle Artist, Author & Photographer.

I AM CANADIAN

BY SUE SUTHERLAND-WOOD

As the first and only member of my family to have been born in Canada, I was always conscious of the fact that although I had a British sentimentality, a tendency to weep with longing over places I had never visited and a bit of an accent myself, these things were mine, tightly stitched into my very anima – and yet not mine. I had one tightly-laced shoe in each country.

This has continued to be true my entire life (brought on in part by four transatlantic moves back and forth) but strangely, and somewhat hilariously, the few negative things my parents used to say about Canada ("They have to put cheese on everything here" or "Any excuse for a party, how *ridiculous* to be making a fuss about – insert banal theme of choice here" or how about "Maple candy? It's that *sweet*! Well, you couldn't *eat it.*") were among the very things I shyly cherished, as a child and an adult.

I longed for the kind of family that, to me, personified being a true Canadian. These people almost always had a cottage that had belonged to their grandparents, or even more distant ancestors who had cleared the land themselves. They participated in outdoorsy activities that seemed incomprehensibly out of reach and deliciously dangerous to me, like boating or chopping wood with an actual axe or cooking "weenies" on a stick over a camp fire. They could be loud and boisterous outside (or even inside!) and no one reprimanded or discouraged them. (Even though this is not peculiar to Canadians, to my young mind it really was). The hospitality, generosity, and genuine kindness was omnipresent – if you were there (perhaps for a "ridiculous party") these folks wanted to make sure you had a good time and felt at home. Under the scorching sun of an Ontario summer, they padded along their own docks often leaping into the clear water, cannon-ball fashion. In winter, they would be out skiing and tobogganing and skidoo-ing (an actual verb in Canada), and huge vats of hot chocolate would later be made for everyone – made the old school way with cocoa and great swirls of cream and condensed milk. I was always the guest and often the observer in many of these activities but I do recall that soft rosy tingle on my skin, a cold so intense that my face glowed from exertion and the uncontrollable laughter that can follow being recently rolled down a hill. I also recall those frozen icy gobbets that winkled their way beneath a pure wool mitten to the wrist and had to be bitten off later when they refused to melt.

(And, can I tell you, as someone who has since been very, very cold in the UK there is nothing to surpass the joy of a Canadian heating vent billowing assertively up your nightwear…)

But I digress. It's not that my parents didn't make an effort, of sorts, to fit in and be more rustic in their own way. But just to be clear, when my British family ate outside during the summer months there were no buckets of chicken in sight; rather, we opted for carrying our meat pie outside. Oh, and someone opened a tin of mandarin oranges for dessert.

My family was also immensely proud of our then cutting-edge 'Canadian' Christmas decorations which featured a bright scarlet string of yellow-haired Mounties holding hands. Their abdomens glowed an eerie dull red when plugged in. We all gathered to admire this key moment each year.

In a similar show of nationalism, each year my father turned his attention to three rectangular raised beds which he "gardened" in. For Canada Day, he would prepare two red beds of petunias and a whitish-red paisley effect in the middle bed to give the sense of the Canadian flag. I helped with this project, but not enthusiastically. In my heart I found the entire effect a little bit lacking and I much preferred the way the park staff had created their own more polished version of the Canadian flag, with rigid begonias and a tighter maple leaf shape that was instantly recognizable. My father's effort was well-intentioned (he could be fiercely patriotic in that grateful, newcomer way) so it's odd that he settled for a gardening display that could well have been paying homage to the Swiss instead.

When my British parents became Canadian citizens I was still a young child. The actual day of the ceremony was filled with pomp and the chanting of solemn promises, as well as gold-edged maple leaf lapel pins and tiny flags to wave. I remember my eyes drifting again and again to a colourful heraldic depiction of a unicorn rampant and a slim-waisted lion showing a long ribbon-like tongue. I noticed they were supporting a shield together. But why were they both so *angry,* I wondered? It troubled me every time I looked back at them to check.

When the judge finally called my parents forward, I went up with them and was suddenly overcome with longing for a piece of this special day. Leaning in, I asked politely and uncertainly if my bear could raise his paw as well. Would this be all right? I could not tell from my parent's eyes if this was going to be construed as charming or more likely, "giving cheek", an offence punishable by death. The judge must have been taken aback because he did not say anything at first so I quickly added, "He's English too! My grandmother sent him to me from England but I think he wants to be Canadian now."

The judge smiled broadly at me and I saw my mother return the smile, so all was well. I held the bear's paw upright in the air and he took the oath with due solemnity, his orange glassy-eyed stare unchanging. I felt that I might burst with pride.

Growing Up Canadian

FIVE ASSISTS

BY MARK KEARNEY

I still remember it.

I'm skating toward the net, shifting my weight as I draw back my stick. My head is down, but as I peer through my badly-fitting helmet, I see an opening in the left side of the net. I shoot, falling to the ice as I follow through.

The goalie kicks out the shot. Wait, it's not over. A teammate skates by and swipes at the rebound, also falling. He shoots, he scores! But the glory is mine. I've just notched the fifth and final assist of my two-year-career as a Tyke hockey player. It didn't elevate me to Gretzky status. But on my team, I was a solid, perhaps even a gifted player. My five assists over two years placed me third among our team's leading scorers.

It began the winter I was eight. Until then, no one my age in my hometown of Pickering, Ontario could play organized hockey, because Pickering was too small a village to justify a Tyke team. But this was now – most of us baby boomers were no longer babies, Pickering Village's population had inched past 1,000 and we wanted more than just backyard rinks. All the big guys, including my brother, were playing organized hockey – it was our turn now.

There was one drawback, besides my mother not wanting her youngest child involved in what she thought was too bone-crushing a sport. Pickering had no arena, and that meant we had to travel some 15 miles to Brooklin, north of Whitby, to practise and play our home games.

In our early practices, under the watchful eye of the coach – who happened to be my father – and the manager, Mr. Dingley, who lived down the street, we tried to skate while wearing pads, and shoot a puck without falling (this was troublesome – "he shoots, he falls" was kind of an unwritten team motto). The previous year I had been my Grade 2 skating champ; that gave me an advantage over some teammates, who despite being young Canadians, tended to have more ankle on the ice surface than blade.

The season started. Perhaps we got thrown into competition too soon. It's difficult to tell when you're eight. Perhaps we hadn't jelled as a team. Perhaps it was the fact that our uniforms, black and orange as I recall, were the product of the benevolent village funeral director, who, of course, didn't object to having his name and service displayed on our jerseys.

We lost our first game 27-0.

Looking back now, the game is a blur. We fell behind early (about 12 seconds after the opening faceoff). I'm not sure what was worse – all those goals, or that most of our team didn't even know the rules. We were lucky not to be called for delay of game as some of our players realized, after a long pause, that they'd lined up in the wrong end of the rink for a faceoff.

After the first period we were down about 14-0.

In the second, we came out with our heads still high (ahh, to be eight again!) and eager for revenge. My father, the coach, told us to shoot the puck into the opposing team's end and skate after it. This was a good strategy, as we had not yet mastered the art of passing. We followed his advice and even managed a few shots on net. It was a good period; we held the opposition to six goals. It may have been after goal 18 flew into our net that I got tired of skating back to our goalie, slapping my stick on his thick pads, and saying "nice try." But my father, the coach, insisted.

A bad fluke game?

No. We lost the next one 21-0 (see above for details).

But the third match was in our arena; Pickering was

going home to Brooklin. During practice we worked on all the things we'd done wrong in the first two games – skating, shooting, goaltending, defence, offence.

Home matches were different. A home game not only meant more cheering fans, but a larger pool of cars to drive us to the arena. When you had someone like my friend Ricky on the team, those extra cars were needed. Ricky wasn't big, but he always wore some part of his equipment to the game. When you're scrunched four or five to a back seat those shoulder pads really cut down on breathing space.

We were playing a team from Cannington, another small Ontario town even farther north of Whitby. And we did improve. Final score: Cannington 15, Pickering 0.

It wasn't the score that was so demoralizing. Heck, keeping the opponents under 20 goals was a major accomplishment. But it was at the 8-0 point when one of the Cannington players skated over to his bench and said "Coach, when can we start trying?"

I had no assists in these games, but that kept me tied for first place in scoring on our team. We suffered through another 27-0 loss in Oshawa, and more lopsided games followed. But the average score was under 20, and we were improving. Certainly our team was starting to line up better for faceoffs.

I guess you always remember your first assist. Halfway through the season we played Sunderland. It became clear late in the first period that our past humiliations weren't going to be repeated; we were only down by three goals. In the second, trailing by about 6-0, my linemate Mick got the puck inside the other team's blue line. He skated toward the net and the puck came loose to me on left wing. I got it to my other linemate John. He shot, fell, and it went in. We'd scored. We rubbed his helmet and started toward the bench. But we were told to stay out there, and amid some scattered applause, the puck was dropped.

Sunderland beat us by about 12-1, but I was on the scoreboard with one assist. Mick and John got a couple of other goals the rest of the year as we finished a perfect first season. No wins, about 20 losses, no ties. My record – no goals, two assists, a couple of penalties. Wait 'til next year, I thought.

We lost next season's opening game 18-0.

Some guys were even crying in the dressing room. Why it took them 21 losses to feel the pain, I don't know. But they recovered. And then – well, I can't lie – we lost every game that season, too. Thanks to the scoring exploits of Mick and John, I racked up another two assists by about halfway through the schedule.

But the best was yet to come – a game against Brooklin.

Two home teams, a Friday night. I didn't feel anything different before the game, but we had played Brooklin before and had always kept them under 10 goals. The score was 3-0 in the second period when Mick skated in on the right side and fired a shot. GOAL!

A few minutes later Mick moved around a defence-man, fired a shot at the goalie, and – Wow! – picked the corner of the net. He raised his arms in triumph, we mobbed him, and the crowd overcame their disbelief and cheered loudly. We were within one. I could feel the rush of adrena-line…or some other bodily fluid. Who knows? I skated harder, hustled to the puck, even threw a body check.

But it wasn't meant to be. We lost 4-2, and I had no assists. Nevertheless, we left the rink in glory, someone patting my shoulder pads and saying "nice game."

My father, the coach, congratulated us, and Mr. Dingley, the manager, treated each of us to a can of pop. I peeled off my jersey (Number 14, the same as my boyhood hero, Dave Keon of the Leafs), sipping a 7Up and joking with my fellow players. My fifth and final assist, the one described at the beginning, was still to come, but in my brilliant hockey career no moment was sweeter than that Friday night in Brooklin.

*My teammates' full names have been left out to save them further embarrassment.

Photo courtesy of Catherine Cocchio

NIAGARA FALLS
VICTORIA DAY
A CANADIAN HERITAGE LESSON

BY CATHERINE COCCHIO

The black and white photo has no date, but fashion clues suggest it was taken in 1958. I'm the little girl in front of our mom. My older sister is beside me, in front of Dad.

You can tell it's windy by the way our matching pleated skirts flap in the breeze. I'm about six years of age, (too young to wear a skirt without straps to hold it up). My sister is proudly sporting the Niagara Falls paper hat provided to children visiting the souvenir shops in town. Dad looks dapper in his suit. Mom looks formal yet relaxed in her crisp spring skirt and blazer. There's probably a cigarette in Dad's left hand. (A habit he gave up cold turkey when my sister was old enough to start smoking).

We are all dressed up in our best clothes because the photo was taken on a Sunday afternoon outing. These outings were very special. My father operated a village grocery store in rural Ontario. He worked long hours and Sunday was his only day off. He loved to drive, so when the weather turned nice in the spring, off we went. You can tell it's early spring. The grass is long, probably not yet cut for the first time. Trees are in full leaf. As a matter of fact, it's Victoria Day weekend. I remember this particular outing since it was an overnight affair with extended family. We would have gone to church and then loaded up the car.

After about three or four hours on two-lane highways, we arrived in Niagara Falls. Following The Parkway along the river, our first stop would have been at Table Rock for a close-up view of the Falls. Unfortunately, the wind must have been in the wrong direction for photography (box cameras were not good in wet conditions) so no photos document the event. Dad continued driving, past the gorge to the floral clock where, well away from the spray, we posed for a family photo.

With lots yet to see, we continued to Queenston where we stopped at the Laura Secord monument. Even though we were far too young to totally understand the significance of the War of 1812, our parents understood the importance of helping us figure out our place in Canadian history by making connections with our roots.

As Dad finished reading the inscription on the monument, he explained why this monument is important to our family. "My grandmother, your great-grandmother, was Martha Secord. Her father Adam was a cousin of Laura Secord," he explained. So that meant we were actually related to a Canadian heroine! Boy, was I surprised!

The history lesson continued at Brock's Monument, where I remember climbing the dark winding stairs. Dad lifted me up to peek out the tiny window at the very top. I also remember that the descent took much less time than the climb, especially once I learned that General Brock was buried at the foot of the monument. (I was afraid of cemeteries.)

The remainder of the holiday is admittedly a bit of a blur. Car travel apparently put me to sleep. I do remember having dinner in a very fancy restaurant on the top floor of the Sheraton Hotel, overlooking the Falls. I had never been in such a tall building, and was impressed at how the cars looked like tiny toys in the parking lot below.

The family spent the night in a motel cabin. Everyone but me enjoyed the light show on the Falls. The weight of the day was too much for me and I fell asleep before the extravaganza began. Holiday Monday's drive home would not have been a quiet one, I'm sure, with plenty of questions about life a century before and observations about how lucky we were to have modern conveniences like telephones and paved roads.

There have been many return trips to Niagara Falls in every season, and every stage of my life. With each visit, the photo tradition continues. Re-creating the original Laura Secord monument pose, I take up my mother's place, standing behind my daughter, with my husband at my side. Our son stands beside his sister, in front of his dad.

Thousands of tourists discover the wonder of Niagara Falls every year, but to our family, the true wonder lies in the deep sense of belonging we experience while there. Firmly planted in the fresh spring turf, our footprints sink deeply into Canadian history. We walk away making our own path, ready to honour old and to create new Canadian traditions.

HOW THE GAME BEGAN

BY NANCY LOUCKS-MCSLOY

I am so excited; it is Grandma's birthday today. Wow, I am four and she is 77 so she must be old. I just like saying "Happy Birthday, Grandma. You are 77 today," because I love saying that number. We are having a little party for Grandma tonight. I wonder what you get for your birthday when you are that old. I know she is going to love the present I am giving her and the card that I drew and coloured for her.

Mommy wants us to hurry and eat our supper so she can clean the kitchen before our company comes. I want to hurry too because I want to go and help Daddy with the chores. It is summer so the cattle are in the pasture and the horse is in the corral. He will just have to feed the pigs, and get the chickens and ducks back into the coop. I want to feed the barn cats and the rabbits. Mommy says no because she doesn't want me to get dirty, but I sneak outside anyway and put supper out for Laddie our dog.

I am sitting with Grandma waiting for the party. Grandma opens her cards that she received in the mail. My aunts and uncles are here with gifts and cards for Grandma. She is given a big bouquet of gladiolas and a new homemade flowered apron, or as Grandma says "a lovely chintz apron." She loves my card and her favourite candies from me.

I look and there is Mr. Dan walking in with a great big package. Mr. Dan is old like Grandma. He always tells me funny stories, and makes things from wood. One day he made me a whistle from a willow branch. He says "Happy Birthday, Mary" and puts the big package by her chair and tells me that I can help Grandma open it. It is not wrapped in pretty wrapping paper, it looks like the paper that Mr. Ed at the general store wraps our meat and groceries in and it is tied with twine.

We carefully take the paper off and I cannot believe my eyes! It is the shiniest, smoothest, most beautiful crokinole board I have ever seen. Mr. Dan made that for Grandma for her birthday. He painted the lines and the numbers on the board and there are even a set of black buttons and a set of white buttons to use. Daddy calls them discs but I think they look like big buttons.

The grownups are going to play cards and crokinole now. I am playing with my dolls Topsy and Rita, but I am watching as the big people start playing crokinole. Soon I am going to put my dolls to bed and then I can sit on Daddy's knee and I know he will let me hit one of those buttons. I bet I will put the button in the center hole. After that we get to have the Devil's Food Cake with fluffy white icing that I helped Mommy make for Grandma.

It is summer 30 years later, and my children are at the family farm near Sauble Beach, visiting Grandma and Grandpa. I call to see how they are doing, but I am quickly told that they can't talk right now because they are playing crokinole. I reminisce about that beautiful, shiny, smooth crokinole board that Mr. Dan made.

Eventually that beautiful crokinole board comes home with us. The kids and their spouses are here along with the grandchildren. They ask to play board games and the suggestion is made that they play crokinole. I watch fondly as my grandchildren sit on their mom's and dad's knees learning how to hit those discs. I realize that the crokinole board that Mr. Dan made has now been passed down through four generations.

Years later I walk through the door of the nineteenth century Port Albert Inn, and to my amazement the wall in the lobby is covered with a collection of vintage crokinole boards. Mark the innkeeper notices my expression and asks if I know anything about crokinole. Of course I do — I grew up with the game. He goes on to tell me that the first crokinole board was made in 1876 in a tiny hamlet in Perth County by Eckhardt Wettlaufer. Mr. Wettlaufer made it for his son, as a gift for his fifth birthday. Mark also talks about how it soon became a popular game in the Mennonite and Amish communities in rural Ontario, as an unoffending substitute for dancing or card playing, which were considered to be somewhat "sinful" by many nineteenth century Protestants, and that Tavistock has been deemed the World Crokinole Capital. I had never really thought of the origin of the game, but now I know that crokinole is another piece of our Canadian heritage.

CENTENNIAL YEAR

BY KYM WOLFE

I had just turned seven and was living in a country that was about to celebrate its 100th birthday. This was a BIG DEAL. On the last day of 1966 my sisters and I had a nap in the afternoon so that we could stay awake to usher in the new year. At midnight we threw open the front door and yelled "Happy New Year" into the frosty Northern Ontario night. Up and down the street people were yelling, banging pots and lids, and generally sending up a cacophony of greetings to Canada's centennial year.

It wasn't until years later, as an adult, that I would understand what a young country Canada was. In my child-like wonder I was enamoured with the pure magic of living in a place that had reached that impressive milestone — 100 years! Imagine! I figured I wouldn't be around to celebrate the bicentennial, so during that brief 12 months I delved into my Canadian roots with pride.

My sister and I learned the song "CA-NA-DA (one little, two little, three Canadians), we love thee...It's the hundredth anniversary of Confederation, ev'rybody sing together! CA-NA-DA..." and would sing it ad nauseum. We built our version of a Centennial symbol in the snow in our front yard, complete with food colouring to outline the different triangles that made up the stylized maple leaf.

Photo courtesy of Kym Wolfe

I read the biographies of each prime minister (beginning with Sir John A. Macdonald and running through to Lester B. Pearson) that appeared each week in the local newspaper, and pasted them carefully into my Centennial Year scrapbook.

I added the specially-minted Canadian coins to my collection and admired the images on the back of each one — the dove of peace on the penny, the rabbit on the nickel, the fish on the dime, the bobcat on the quarter and the Canada goose on the dollar. I never did manage to find a 50-cent piece to complete my collection, but I did put a paper dollar bill carefully into a plastic sleeve and saved it in my treasure box — I would run across it years later and recall how cool it had seemed to my seven-year-old eyes, and wonder at how disciplined I must have been to not spend it.

I also collected the coins given away by Shell with every gas fill-up (thanks Dad!) — one for every province and territory, sporting the coat-of-arms on one side and the official flower on the other side, plus a Canada coin with the national coat-of-arms and maple leaf embossed on it. "A Mari usque ad Mare" — From Sea to Sea, I read, and I traced the line of provinces across the globe, stretching from the Atlantic to the Pacific, and north to the Arctic Ocean. One day, I vowed, I would travel from one end to the other.

When Queen Juliana came to Canada to celebrate the Tulip Festival, I learned that part of Ottawa was, for a brief time, not part of Canada. After the Nazis invaded the Netherlands, the Dutch royal family came to live in Canada for the duration of World War II. When Princess Juliana gave birth in Ottawa Civic Hospital in 1943, the Canadian government temporarily declared the maternity ward to be extraterritorial (technically international territory outside of the Canadian domain), so that the newborn Princess Margriet was born with purely Dutch citizenship. After returning home in 1945, the royal family sent Ottawa 10,000 tulip bulbs. It's become an annual tradition, leading to a spring Tulip Festival that has been celebrated annually since 1953.

Perhaps my most haunting memory from that year comes from our visit to the Confederation Train. When it rolled into Sault Ste. Marie I stood in line and boarded it to explore the cars that had special interactive exhibits, each highlighting part of Canada's history. The one I remember most clearly is the car that had been transformed into a war-time trench, with the wounded groaning in their bunks and artillery fire flashing beyond the gaps in the sand bags — a terrifying experience that hit too close to home, because even at that young age I had some awareness that my grandfather and uncles had served in the war.

The fireworks on July 1 that year were, of course, amazing. I understood in some way that this was Canada's year to shine on the world stage. I read about Expo 67, which drew visitors from around the globe to Montreal and is still considered one of the 20th century's most successful World's Fairs. The next year my parents took us to Man and His World, where we visited the Expo pavilions that had not been dismantled. My favourite by far was one that seemed to be filled with all kinds of things to climb over, bounce on and slide down — I could have stayed for days.

Years later, when I learned that we would be pulling out all the stops to celebrate Canada's sesquicentennial, I was filled once again with a sense of excitement. Would there be a new CA-NA-DA song to sing? Would there be a new Centennial train to visit? Although I don't view the celebrations with the same wonderment I felt in 1967, I hope that some seven-year-old somewhere across the country will. But I still feel that enormous sense of pride in my home and native land. Happy 150th Birthday, Canada!

HOME AGAIN

BY EVELYN SYMONS

It was only an hour-and-a-half drive, but the journey would have an enormous impact on the rest of my life. I was 10. Our family of nine (including the dog and cat) left the city of Richmond Hill, Ontario where my father had been an advertising executive for radio station CFGM, which in 1967 had a country and western format. For me, this was move number four.

With a grey tabby cat and a large golden dog on my lap, I watched the scenery change from the backseat window. The highway became a quiet country road that dipped and meandered, often following streams and rivers. It was County Road 9 of the Nottawasaga Township that took us to our new home, The Dunedin General Store. Life in the city was now in the rear view mirror.

The four doors of our midnight blue Oldsmobile Delta 88 opened simultaneously, all for different reasons. My mom had had a baby on her knee for the duration of the car ride; my father was to meet with the previous owner,

Bruce Leighton, and my oldest brother was probably on the lookout for pretty girls. My door was barely open when the cat leapt from the car, followed by Susie, my collie-shepherd mix. It was time to explore our new surroundings.

I ran into the house through the side door of the enclosed porch, known afterwards as the mudroom. Only the kitchen's pale green swinging door separated the house from the general store. The room was enormous with lots of light streaming in the windows. A black wall-mounted telephone rang from across the empty kitchen.

The ring sounded different than the one I was used to – there were two long rings, and one short one. I picked up the receiver and said hello. A firm female voice quickly questioned me, asking "Where's Doreen?" She had me there. I had no idea who Doreen was, let alone where she was. I explained that I was the new girl moving into the store. Her voice softened as she gently chastised me. "You must wait for your own ring before you answer the phone, dear." Still not understanding, I said "Oh." I even nodded my head, as if she could see me. That was my introduction to the party line.

The Noisy River ran through our backyard. It was a fast-moving river that cascaded over rocks, and was so close that if you lost hold of your laundry while hanging it out on a windy day, it could very well end up making its way downstream toward the Nottawasaga River.

The hamlet of Dunedin is one of the many valleys tucked into the Niagara Escarpment. To me, that meant summer hills to hike and winter hills to toboggan. I was in heaven.

Susie became a country dog and no longer had to be tied up. She and I could walk for miles, and we did. I signed on to be the neighbourhood papergirl. With my canvas bag slung across my tall slender frame, I walked for two hours each day delivering 12 Toronto Telegram newspapers to homes and farms. The farthest farm belonged to the Royals and on the hot days of summer Mrs. Royal would see to it that I had a cold glass of lemonade before my walk home.

I read any extra papers dropped off in the bundle on the front porch of the store. I read about the love affair many Canadians had with Pierre Elliot Trudeau, and about Steven Truscott being denied a second trial. (Thankfully in 2007, he was acquitted of all charges.) Two of my customers faithfully rewarded me each Saturday with a 10 cent tip; this gesture from Mr. Felstead and Mr. George Scriver always made me feel very special. I later learned that Mr. Scriver was an inventor at heart. In 1916 he invented an automobile tire pump that ran off the car's engine. That was a big deal back then, with road conditions less than ideal. I can still see this quiet, slender man standing in his doorway, perhaps waiting for the arrival of a lanky girl and her dog.

I quickly learned that many people were related to each other and I did my best to learn everyone's name. There were Royals, Rowbothams, Weatheralls, Hallidays, Hammills, Youngs, Abbeys, Meatherals and many more. One Mrs. Meatheral was now my Grade 5 teacher and the school principal. I didn't hear her once raise her voice. She lived in the white house set back from the road at the end of the village, just as it heads to Creemore where the school was. It was a school bus ride away.

Each school day, the bus passed the store and headed to the farthest farm to pick up Marc Royal along with Janet and Alan Abbey. I could watch it from my upstairs bedroom window and knew I had a few more minutes before I would be boarding from the front porch with my lunchbox in hand. I loved my new lunchbox. I loved it even more when my mother packed a big juicy orange — it made a wonderful trade for the delicious chocolate cake that Janice Walker's mother packed for her.

Along with being the new storeowner, my father assumed the role of postmaster, as each store proprietor had done since 1869. He sorted the mail just as you would imagine, putting letters into the wooden cubbies that were the backdrop of our tiny post office located inside the store. It was closed in 1969 (Creemore Post office assumed the responsibility) making my father the last postmaster of a 100-year-old tradition.

Our home was filled with adventure. The kitchen pipes froze; my older sister started to date; my oldest brother fell in love (with the girl he's still married to); I caught a younger brother smoking with a friend at the age of six, and another younger brother somehow locked himself out on a balcony for a few hours. The kitchen doubled as the living room for a short time, while my father turned the living room into a Yamaha motorcycle showroom before extending the building. I wonder if the extension was my mother's idea?

We watched Hockey Night in Canada, when our rooftop aerial and the weather would allow. I tobogganed the hills, walked the river's edge, and swam in the swimming hole. I played baseball in the park on the other side of the river. It was an automatic home run if you could hit the ball into the river.

There were several more moves in my future. My parents worried. Did they move the family too many times? Would their five children ever feel that they had roots, after the many transplants? Would they ever feel at home?

They needn't have worried. The move to Dunedin

helped me to realize that I am home in the city or the country, standing near the ocean, or enjoying the company of old and new friends, wherever they live. Home is in the imagining of my mother's hug or my father's next big plan. For it is not a physical location − home is a state of mind, a wonderful feeling. Home is where we feel safe to be who we are. It is where we feel joy, and warmth and love. Home is where we never feel less-than. It is fun. It's where we laugh as loud as we want, or cry without feeling small.

My home looks like freedom. It is a safe place to launch toward the next adventure. And when I lose my way, home feels even better. I am home again.

Travels
Near and Far

A HERO IN ANY LANGUAGE

BY CHRISTOPHER CLARK

I lost my wallet one summer day sometime in the mid-1980s.

Given the paucity of facts in that statement, it's difficult to believe I could have gotten one wrong, but to be accurate, the wallet was not lost, but stolen, from my unlocked car in Oshawa.

Back then, people stole tangible things like cars, stereos and TVs – not identities. I'm sure I had to call in and tell someone my credit card was gone, but I'm equally certain I didn't have to remember the middle names of all my grade school teachers to get a replacement. The only password I had was the four-digit code for my bank card, which was just as simple to replace as the card itself. So I didn't have to spend the following week updating passwords, reconfiguring profiles and assuring disembodied voices in faraway lands I was who I said I was.

The wallet itself had no sentimental value. In fact, later that summer when the police called to tell me it had been found 10 minutes from my house, ditched next to a creek, I didn't bother to go pick it up. The cash was gone. The credit and bank cards were gone. There was only one thing I had been sorry to lose, and the friendly officer on the phone confirmed it was not in the wallet.

The thing I missed was a small newspaper clipping from 1981. It had been there for a handful of years and was pretty tattered. Not only that, it was in German, so I couldn't actually read it. But I knew what it said. And I remembered exactly when I clipped it and placed it in my wallet. It represented perhaps the greatest loss I had felt to that point in my life, at the tender age of 15.

I was in Germany on June 28, 1981, when Terry Fox died. News travelled differently then. The process was slower, yes, but not exactly slow. Wire services delivered the story to European news agencies within hours. And the next day it appeared as a small item in the newspaper that arrived at the house in Wangen, where I was staying.

I was one of 60 high school students on a two-week band trip, billeting with families as we made our way around Germany and Austria, playing concerts for curious passers-by, and pairing up like passengers on Noah's ark during our free time.

Even with the language barrier, my week living with

the family in Wangen was wonderful. It turns out ping pong is a universal language. Early in my stay, the father of the house got out an atlas (no password required) and displayed a large map of North America. With hand gestures and some rudimentary English, he asked, innocently, if Canada and the United States were, practically speaking, just one big country.

I turned to the map of Europe and shook my head, full of teenage confidence and indignation. Unaware of the geopolitical faux pas I was committing, I waved my hand over several countries, including what was then West Germany, and asked if all of this was really just one country. "Nein, nein, nein," he said with more emotion than my naïve self expected. He turned back to North America, and gestured with both hands his newfound understanding that Canada was quite separate from the United States, no matter how similar they might appear from the other side of the Atlantic.

Later in the week, the father showed me the Terry Fox story in that day's newspaper. There was a picture of Terry in action, running his Marathon of Hope, and about six column-inches of story. "What does it say?" I asked with some anxiety.

"Dead," the father said, closing his eyes to make the point. I didn't cry until later.

Knowing full well the father could not understand

much of what I was saying, I launched into a five-minute monologue about what Terry Fox meant to Canada. To me.

We had been told numerous times by the parents who had come with us on the trip that we were representing Canada while there – that our behaviour should reflect that. But only in that moment did I actually feel like I was representing my country to the people of another.

I told the father how Terry started his run on the east coast, how he dipped his artificial leg in the Atlantic and planned to dip it in the Pacific several months later. I told him how he ran the equivalent of a marathon every day, initially in near anonymity. I told him how the country soon rallied around him, how newspapers sent reporters and photographers to travel with him and tell the world about what he was doing. I told him that cities and towns of all sizes welcomed him along his route, holding rallies with speeches and brass bands and bake sales.

I told him that by the time Terry got to Ontario, his route was almost always lined with people who clapped and cheered and cried. How he met with children fighting cancer everywhere he went. How the prime minister welcomed him in Ottawa. How thousands flooded city hall in Toronto to support him.

But mostly I told him about the day he arrived in

Oshawa. The day my mother took my younger brothers and me to the Oshawa Centre shopping mall. How we lined up with hundreds of people as he ran through the mall. It felt like Superman had come to our town.

And I told him, finally, about the day Terry stopped his run, near Thunder Bay, after 143 days and more than 5,300 kilometres. The damned disease was back, this time in his lungs. It was the only thing that could force him off the road and back home for treatment. A week later, a national telethon celebrated Terry's accomplishment, raised millions more dollars for cancer research, and served as a thank-you from a grateful nation. On that night, Canadians were in denial, praying to their various gods that Terry would somehow recover a second time and be able to continue his Marathon.

But it wasn't to be.

The father listened to me, understanding, if not every detail, at least the fact that a national hero had died and that millions were grieving. Then he found some scissors so I could cut out the article. It was the most meaningful souvenir I brought home from the trip.

When our band assembled for the day's activities, nearly everyone had heard. And nearly everyone had gone through a similar series of events at the homes where they were staying. We were 60 ambassadors for Canada, explaining not just the headline news back home but also the emotional toll it was taking on 24 million people.

It would be lovely to say we dedicated the rest of the trip to Terry or that he was in our minds for the remaining nine or ten days. I remember our conductor at that day's concerts telling the crowds what had happened and why it was so important to the group of Canadians they were about to hear play.

But we were teenagers on the adventure of a lifetime, and we quickly reverted to the hormonal, prank-playing goof-offs we actually were. We missed the funeral, which was broadcast across Canada. We weren't home to see flags flying at half-mast nationwide.

We experienced his death in a unique setting and relied on each other for story-telling and support.

The newspaper clipping reminded me of all that. It reminded me of how proud I was to be a Canadian on the terrible day when news of Terry's death circled the globe. It reminded me of those few moments with the German father, pouring out my story to someone who was kind enough to listen and understand. And it will always remind me of the summer day in 1980 when a flesh-and-blood hero came to our town.

Photo by Kym Wolfe

THE FUR-BEARING TROUT

BY KYM WOLFE

I n 1982 I was sitting in the subway — or should I say the Tube? — in London, England when I spied a familiar fish. "Can't be!" I thought. So I leaned in to take a closer look at the transit ad. Sure enough, it *was* a picture of a fish — one that I had seen every summer for years, hanging on a wall in a camp in Canada.

Northern Ontario cottages are often referred to as camps. Especially rustic cottages like the one owned by my in-laws. It was equipped with an outhouse, and the only running water was drawn straight from Lake Superior. The camp was a wonderful place to visit, and the walls were decorated with a mix of cool things — including a plaqued Fur-Bearing Trout that had been created by an in-town neighbour, Mr. Jobe.

Mr. Jobe was a First Nations fellow who owned a huge piece of property in Sault Ste. Marie, Ontario. My husband had grown up right across the street from it, and I'd heard stories about the many wonders of Jobe's Bush. The outdoor rink, complete with boards and lights, where the neighbourhood kids would skate and play hockey all winter and warm up by the pot-bellied, wood-burning stove in the rink shack. The carved totem pole that stretched 15 or 20 feet high, with a rope hanging down from the top — if you were tall enough to jump up and grab the bottom of the rope, you could climb all the way up. The end-of-school bonfire, when all of the kids would bring their notebooks and papers to burn in the wooden model schoolhouse that Mr. Jobe had constructed. And the wood shop where Mr. Jobe carved Indian heads and assembled his Fur-Bearing Trout.

Each 'trout' was fashioned by hand from a piece of rabbit skin to which Mr. Jobe attached a fish head, fins and tail. He'd mount it on a piece of wood with these words below it:

FUR BEARING TROUT

Very Rare

CAUGHT WHILE TROLLING IN LAKE SUPERIOR OFF
GROS CAP, NEAR SAULT STE. MARIE,
DISTRICT OF ALGOMA

It is believed that the great depth and the extreme penetrating
coldness of the water in which these fish live, has caused them
to grow their dense coat of
(usually) white fur.
Mounted by ROSS C. JOBE,
Taxidermist of Sault Ste. Marie, Ont.

A lot of tourists bought Mr. Jobe's Fur-Bearing Trout, and one gullible guy presented one to the Royal Museum in Edinburgh, Scotland. It was a treasured part of the museum's collection — until someone figured out that they had swallowed a tall tale — hook, line and sinker! Years later, that's what I was reading about on the transit posting in the Tube. The Fur-Bearing Trout was cited as one of the great unintentional museum hoaxes.

To a Canadian who had just arrived in London, it was an interesting tidbit to run across. What, I wondered, do the Brits think of their colonial cousins when they read stories like this? How do other Europeans view us? I was about to learn.

It was an eye-opening experience to have Canada's reputation reflected back to me through the people that I met. Maybe it was a foolish thing, since I had had no control over where I was born, but during those few months of travelling I often felt a swell of pride in being Canadian.

In a Munich beer garden I learned that Canada's King of Polka, Walter Ostanek, was a renowned entertainer in Germany. People were gobsmacked to learn that I didn't know his music and had never seen his band perform.

A pub owner in Scotland felt a kinship because she had experienced a 'Canadian' winter during 1978-79, one of the worst winters on record in Great Britain. She pulled out a photo album to show us pictures of her husband, shovel in hand, standing on their front walkway between snow banks piled higher than his head.

In Barcelona we got off the well-worn tourist track and had dinner in a small restaurant frequented by locals. The owner was so thrilled to have Canadian visitors that after dinner he pulled out his wineskin — well-used, obviously well-loved — and treated us to his personal stash of sangria.

We were afforded a warm welcome and friendly respect by Dutch people who had never met us, but had grown up knowing that in WWII it was Canadian soldiers who had liberated the Netherlands.

When we crossed from Greece into Turkey and got off the bus to stretch our legs, the women sporting visible maple leaf pins were immediately surrounded by young men professing their love and asking us to marry them. To wangle a Canadian wife and be able to move to our country — for them that would be akin to winning the lottery.

The only place my Canadianness got any disrespect was in Bulgaria, where merchants turned up their noses at my Canadian traveller's cheques; they would only accept US dollars. Later, as we rolled through the countryside and I saw a man walking behind his mule to hand-till his field, I recognized the demand for American currency was driven purely by practicality.

There I was, a recent university graduate, saddled with student debt, living out of a knapsack, sleeping in a tent, and travelling on a shoestring budget. But I could count myself among the world's most fortunate and wealthy, simply because I had been born Canadian. It was a humbling realization — purely by accident, my winning lottery numbers had aligned at birth.

My sense was that most of the world looked favourably upon Canadians. We were caring, polite, respectful and not too demanding. We were talented musicians, brave soldiers, and loyal allies. We were toque-wearing, hardy souls who could brave the elements. We produced the world's best maple syrup and hockey players. And we had a sense of humour. After all, if anyone needed proof of our finely tuned funny bone, well — they need only take a look through the archives at a certain museum in Scotland, eh?

HOOKED ON TRAVEL BY RAIL

BY JOHNNY FANSHER

I t's a big year for Canada and me. Being born in 1967 didn't mean much to me as a child when adults would tell me I am a centennial baby; but 50 years later, when Canada is celebrating its 150th, there is something very special about sharing milestone birthdays with my home and native land.

I feel very fortunate to have been born a Canadian. Whenever I travel abroad, which I do as often as I can, identifying myself as a Canadian regularly attracts favourable interactions. I have come to believe that Canadians are admired all over the world because we are known for being friendly and progressive.

On a trip to Scotland during the spring of 2010, I experienced an "Aha!" moment on a rail journey through the Scottish Highlands. Realizing how much I enjoy leisure travel by train, I noted in my journal, "I must see Canada by rail."

With Canada's rail lines having been built over a century ago to connect our nation from coast to coast, I knew that I needed to make the entire journey. Almost exactly a year later, in the spring of 2011, I booked a cabin for one on board VIA Rail's *The Canadian* departing from Toronto en route to Vancouver.

Initially I contemplated starting at one coast and travelling by train to the other, but because my home, in London, Ontario, is conveniently located on VIA's Windsor/Quebec corridor, it made more sense to set off from there, travelling by train from London to Toronto to Vancouver, flying from Vancouver to Halifax, then travelling by train once more westward from Halifax back to London.

I fondly remember my experience of boarding *The Canadian* at Toronto's Union Station. I felt like a little boy on the inside, which must have been evident to everyone around me because I took complete delight in exploring everything on board and sharing my enthusiasm with other travellers.

My sleeping car happened to be adjacent to the Park Car at the tail end of the train, a stroke of good fortune because I spent most of my waking hours engaging with other guests inside the Park Car's Bullet Lounge, or upstairs on the observation deck, or downstairs in the Mural Lounge.

On that first night, I made friends with a man named Joran, from Alkmaar in the Netherlands. Like so many of the foreign passengers on board, Joran had heard from his travel agent that the best way to see Canada was by train. He was loving the experience as much as I was. Together, over the days to follow, we met just about everyone on board, discovering tourists from Europe, Britain, Australia, Asia and the United States, as well as other Canadians.

The first full day on board took us through northern Ontario, giving me my first glimpse of the breathtaking landscapes of the Canadian Shield. Every moment seemed like a picturesque opportunity to capture photos of lakes and trees, more lakes and trees and, as the hours passed, even more lakes and trees. I never grew tired of it.

Our second full day commenced with an early morning arrival into Winnipeg, the longest stop throughout the journey. Here the entire crew changes over and passengers have nearly four hours to explore the city.

Prior to taking this trip, I was told by naysayers that I would probably be bored to tears as I travelled through the prairies. Simply not true!

Travelling alongside the Assiniboine River Valley throughout southwestern Manitoba, and its tributary the Qu'Appelle River, in southeastern Saskatchewan, was a beautiful experience. Even when the train tracks veered northwest away from the riverbanks and into the prairie flatlands, there was a rolling landscape that was beautiful in its own right. That evening while heading northwest through Saskatchewan en route to Saskatoon we were graced with a magnificent prairie sunset.

Our third full day commenced with an early morning arrival on the outskirts of Edmonton, Alberta. This last segment being the most breathtaking and popular part of the journey, the train powered down for about an hour while new sleeping cars and a panorama car were added.

By midafternoon, as we came to Hinton, Alberta, the Rockies were beginning to reveal their majesty. In short order, we arrived at Jasper for a nearly two-hour stop. What an astonishingly beautiful place. It was fascinating to watch caribou wandering through the village and awe-inspiring to realize that Jasper National Park belonged more to its abundant wildlife than it did to us; we were merely visitors.

As we departed Jasper that afternoon, the rest of the day was nothing short of extraordinary, with magnificent landscape throughout the duration of our journey through Alberta and into British Columbia. The Rockies are a must-see for all Canadians.

On the fourth day our train arrived in the late morning at Vancouver's Pacific Central Station.

After a week in Vancouver (I always feel like there's never enough time to see and spend time in the beautiful west coast city) and two flights later, I landed in Halifax. This was my first time setting foot in the province of Nova Scotia and, although I am tempted to tell about my adventures there during the Victoria Day weekend, I'm going to stay on track – pun intended.

The rail journey from Halifax to Montreal on board VIA's *The Ocean* takes less than 24 hours, paling somewhat in comparison to *The Canadian*'s three-and-a-half day journey.

The equipment on *The Ocean* is quite different than *The Canadian's,* so once again I explored the entire train, feeling like a kid all over again. The biggest difference was the layout of the sleeping cars. For starters, there are no cabins for one on board *The Ocean* so I got a cabin for two with no single supplement upcharge – bonus!

There were many beautiful vistas to enjoy while traveling along the Bedford Basin on our way out of Halifax, and I was especially moved by the beauty of the Baie des Chaleurs between Bathurst and Campbellton, New Brunswick.

At dinner that night, rather than having dessert, I requested an extra bowl of seafood chowder. Yes, it was really that good! I won't go on at length about my many extraordinary experiences of dining on board *The Canadian* and *The Ocean*, but will sum it all up by saying there was nothing quite like being called to the dining car thrice daily to be served chef-prepared gourmet meals, served on china, set atop white linen.

Every menu offered up several amazing choices and included options to satisfy all of the particular palates and preferences of discerning diners. Canadian specialties and popular regional dishes often reflected the area that the train was travelling through at the moment.

The next morning, rather than continue all the way to Montreal, I stopped over in Quebec City for two nights. It is one of my favourite places in the world. Quebec City is Canada's Europe; rich in culture and heritage and full of architectural masterpieces.

After two nights in Quebec I took a corridor train to Montreal for a night, and then another to Toronto for a night, and then finally another home to London. Each destination would be worthy of a tale in its own right.

Within a year of committing to see my country by train, I had made my wish come true, and I got hooked on long-haul train travel by doing so.

I have since taken *The Canadian* five times westward or eastward, in all seasons, and have once experienced *The Skeena*, which travels from Jasper, Alberta to Prince Rupert, British Columbia. I love British Columbia during springtime because it's as colourful as the land of Oz.

During the summer months, the purple flax and yellow canola fields scattered across the prairies are as eye-catching as the tulip fields of the Netherlands are in springtime.

Nothing beats autumn in Ontario, with the diverse colours of changing maple trees. Although it was amazing to witness the colonies of aspen turning chartreuse against the dark green deciduous forests of Alberta.

Winter paints its white and icy brushstrokes differently all across Canada. The northern Ontario lakes freeze over, becoming popular for ice fishing tourism, and there is nothing like snow-covered peaks for winter sports enthusiasts.

I've come to realize that there are a lot of regulars who travel annually across Canada by train. Three times I've crossed paths with passengers I've met before. It's always a joy to reconnect with crew and to keep meeting tourists from all over the world.

To celebrate Canada's 150th and my 50th I have once again booked a cabin on board *The Canadian,* and this spring will travel from Toronto to Vancouver. This time I have planned a two-night stopover in Winnipeg to visit good friends who recently relocated there. I feel as excited

as ever about the prospect of yet another journey by rail
westward across our great nation.

All aboard!

Photo by Mark Kearney

The Canadian War Memorial at Vimy Ridge in northern France was an inspiring venue for the adult members of the Don Wright Faculty of Music New Horizons Band.

PLAYING IN THE SHADOW OF VIMY

BY MARK KEARNEY

Shouts of "Encore!" in Paris, the palpable feeling of dignity while performing at the Vimy Memorial, and a standing ovation in the Netherlands. My 2007 trip to Europe was not typical, but like most of our life journeys it had moments that overwhelmed any overall sense of destination.

I play second clarinet in the Don Wright Faculty of Music New Horizons Band here in London, Ontario. It sounds more impressive than it should. Essentially, we are a group of adult players, many of whom began, as beginners, a few years earlier and who perform at high school band level. What we may lack in musicianship we more than make up for in chutzpah.

This was our band's second European "tour", having played free concerts in Prague, Vienna and Budapest two years previously. On this trip we played in Paris, Vimy, Bruges and Amsterdam, with one of those venues being the grounds outside the palace at Versailles. Hey, go big or go home.

As fun as it was playing for the passersby at Versailles, that wasn't the moment that resonated most for me; three others were more satisfying.

The first occurred in Paris's Luxembourg Gardens where we played outdoors under the threat of ominous clouds. We had a small roof over our heads in the pavilion where we set up, but the audience that gathered had no such protection. We managed to stay rain free for our first few songs.

When the rain hit, I knew I wasn't the only band

member thinking "uh-oh, everybody's going to leave." But to our delight and surprise, the audience opened their umbrellas and stayed. They applauded enthusiastically for each number and one man shouted, "Encore, encore!"

It felt good, even though one band member immediately leaned over and said, "don't forget, the French like Jerry Lewis." But our exuberant fan's shouts were still music to my ears, even when I learned later that he had been guzzling wine throughout the concert and likely wanted musical accompaniment to help him finish the bottle.

Vimy was as solemn as Paris had been raucous. The opportunity to visit the Vimy Memorial was perhaps the key reason people signed up for the trip this time – to play at the memorial during the 90th anniversary year of that famous battle. There wasn't much of a crowd that day, but we didn't care. We would have played to empty fields in the driving rain, if it had come to that. Instead, we had sunny, windy weather and a small audience – friends who accompanied us on the tour, a few curious onlookers touring the site and several sheep grazing nearby.

A few band members mentioned afterward how emotional they felt playing in the memorial's shadow. One song in particular, "Nightfall in Camp", chosen specifically for the Vimy concert, proved challenging for those caught up in its significance. For me, it was "O Canada" that set off the emotion. I'm not a big admirer of anthems played at virtually every gathering, but this was different. About two notes in I felt my throat clutch and thought, "Jeez, I'm playing 'O Canada' at Vimy. Get it right."

Seeing the Vimy Memorial on TV, as so many Canadians did during the 100th anniversary in 2017, is simply not the same as being there in person. It is a remarkable site that first captivates your eyes and then ultimately your heart.

The third resonant moment came at our concert in Zeist, near Amsterdam. Our audience there wasn't just people sauntering by; this outdoor theatre's bleachers were filled with fans that had come specifically to hear us play. Our band's photo was in their summer program alongside a blurb about our coming from Canada to perform just for them. They wanted us to play two sets, with an intermission, as if we were, you know, real musicians. They normally didn't hold concerts on Monday evenings, but for us they made an exception.

No pressure.

But we managed. It may not have been our strongest performance but it was solid enough. The audience seemed to enjoy our efforts and, to our astonishment, gave us a standing ovation. Take that, Jerry Lewis.

I know I'll never be another Benny Goodman, no matter how much I practise, but the joy comes from those rare times when either the listeners truly appreciate what you're trying to do or the band finds its unity in the sweep of a few notes that somehow sound ... exactly right. That's my memory of Zeist.

There were also non-musical moments from this tour that still resound. Standing in a room in Anne Frank's House in Amsterdam, looking up at the attic where she would sometimes seek solace. The gathering of a few band members late one evening near the Eiffel Tower sharing chocolate, bottles of wine, and waggish remarks. Silently strolling through the Canadian cemetery at Vimy seeing so many graves inscribed with the words "A soldier of the Great War Known unto God."

But those moments deserve their own stories.

GIANT THINGS AND OTHER SCRAPS OF TRIVIA

BY KYM WOLFE

In 1967 I celebrated Canada's centennial year with wonderment of a seven-year-old, reveling at the excitement and silently vowing that one day I would see the length and breadth of this amazing country, from the Atlantic to the Pacific.

Eventually I dipped my foot into the Pacific Ocean at Tofino, and a few years later posed for a picture at Cape Spear, Newfoundland. It had taken almost 50 years of patchwork travel, but finally I had indeed seen my home and native land "A Mari Usque ad Mare", From Sea to Sea. And I had seen it by car, except for the short stretch from the Okanagan Valley to Vancouver.

For some unknown reason, my mind tends to trap trivia, scraps of knowledge that take up space in my memory bank. Here are some of the things that have stuck with me from my coast-to-coast travels.

Canadians like to build giant things. As a girl growing up in Northern Ontario I had seen the Big Nickel towering over the then-desolate landscape of Sudbury, and the enormous Canada Goose statue at Wawa. Later in life, on a family holiday to the Maritimes, I was delighted to discover the Giant Lobster in Shediac, New Brunswick and a towering stack of three goofy-faced blueberries in Oxford, Nova Scotia.

Until I visited Gimli, Manitoba I had no idea that Canada has the largest population of Icelandic people outside of Iceland. In 1875 the Government of Canada granted land for an Icelandic Reserve on the west shore of Lake Winnipeg, in the wilderness of the North-West Territories. The settlers in "New Iceland" enjoyed political autonomy, creating their own laws, running their own schools, and generally managing their own affairs until 1881, when Manitoba's borders were extended north and New Iceland fell under provincial jurisdiction. The residents of Gimli ardently embrace their Icelandic roots, and this is where I encountered Canada's giant Viking statue.

More recently I discovered the world's Largest Fiddle while waiting to board the ferry in Cape Breton Island, and took a detour off the highway at Nackawic to see the World's Largest Axe, a tribute to New Brunswick's forestry industry (truth be told, it was the Big Axe craft brewery that swayed my decision). And guess what, New York? You might have the name, but we actually have the world's Big Apple here in Ontario! From BC's huge Hockey Stick to Newfoundland's Giant Squid, and dozens of points in between, we are a nation that has created massive monuments to capture elements of our history and culture.

I've also taken note of the streak of altruism that seems to run through our history. I think it's an admirable trait, and I'm guessing that the more than 6,000 passengers whose planes were bound for New York but diverted to Gander on September 11, 2001 would agree. I came across another shining example when I visited Banting House and learned that when Frederick Banting and his team introduced insulin to the world in 1923 – wanting to ensure that it would be mass produced and distributed – they patented their discovery and promptly sold the rights to the University of Toronto for $1 each ($3 in total) with the proviso that pharmaceutical companies would be allowed to manufacture insulin royalty-free, to ensure it would remain affordable for anyone who needed it.

We may not brag a lot about our homegrown dis-coveries, but we're a pretty clever bunch. If you use a paint roller or a snow blower, feed your baby Pablum, drink Bloody Caesars, eat poutine, enjoy basketball, or protect your face with a goalie mask – thank a Canadian.

Some of our inventions and adaptations are more practical than others, born of necessity. We can thank Canada's indigenous people for the birch bark canoe, described by early explorers as the only craft suited to navigate the waterways of the Canadian Shield. I grew up riding snowmobiles as a leisure sport, but the first Ski-Doos were used by trappers, prospectors and missionaries to travel to remote areas that were only accessible by dog sled in the winter (apparently Bombardier named his invention the Ski-Dog, but the company brochure went to print with the spelling error, and the name Ski-Doo stuck).

During a wine tour in Prince Edward County I learned that the vintners there pioneered a technique to enable them to grow chardonnay, pinot and other traditionally European vines which would not normally survive a harsh Canadian winter. Even Alexander Graham Bell, best known for inventing the telephone, eventually turned his hand to agricultural innovation, as I discovered when I visited his estate near Baddeck on Cape Breton Island. Bell bred sheep with extra nipples, hoping it would result in more twins being born to those ewes, and eventually provide farmers with a means to double their flocks. There is no record of how successful he was.

Canada is big, and our landscape is diverse, which you really notice if you travel by road or by rail. When we visited family in Calgary we drove to Banff one day and rode the gondola high into the Rocky Mountains. The next day we drove east into the flatness of the prairies, wheat silos, and the endless miles of uninterrupted horizon that provided an incredibly beautiful sunset.

We have some fairly unique geographical features, like the stands of sugar maples that supply the world with Canadian maple syrup or the massive red cedars that we saw in Vancouver Island's Cathedral Grove. But others reflect a kinship to other sites around the globe. In Gros Morne National Park we took a boat ride through a fjord that is said to be as picturesque as those in Norway. Alexander Graham Bell built a home in the Bras d'Or Lake area because it reminded him of his Scottish homeland. The "singing sands" at Basin Head in PEI (which, to be honest, sounded more like squeaking than singing) share a phenomenon with select beaches around the globe. The surf at Tofino is said to rival that of Big Sur (although the surfers we saw all wore wet suits – our water is much more frigid).

And we have a diversity of people, most of whom have found their way here as immigrants, going back to the early 1600s. Each wave of newcomers has influenced our country, and many have brought traditions, foods and customs that have been passed down from one generation to the next.

A passionate pride in our roots is a common thread that I've seen running through Canadian communities across the country. Although the heritage that is being celebrated or honoured may be totally different, I've witnessed the same sense of pride, whether I was sitting by a campfire on the shores of Lake Superior, or watching dancers and drummers at a First Nations pow wow, or drinking "moose milk" at a military mess, or taking a guided historical walking tour, or being honoured with an Ethiopian coffee ceremony.

My sense is that we are like this big group of unique siblings – we can poke fun at ourselves and grumble a bit at each other, but we'll be fiercely loyal to the whole family if push comes to shove. At least, that's my hope for this wonderful country that I proudly call home.

THE GREAT OUTDOORS

DAY SIX

BY MELANIE CHAMBERS

The sound of a snapping twig startles me awake and I almost fall backwards from the branch that I've been sitting on all night. Shifting my weight to steady myself, deep indents from the bark are embedded in my thighs and tree sap is smeared across my forehead from resting on the tree.

Straddling the line between consciousness and sleep, I can't tell what is real. The snapping below gets louder.

The forest echoes with crunching. I know it's the bear. It's been following me all day and now it's under my dangling feet. Peering out between the branches, I see the full moon on the horizon giving the tree tips a silver glow. On any other night this would be beautiful.

Lost in a 56,000-hectare forest in British Columbia's South Chicouton Mountains, with a bear stalking me.

Who takes off into the woods without telling anyone? I do. Friends at home wouldn't be surprised, 'this is classic Melanie.' Spontaneous, impulsive, free spirited — the first one to jump into a lake without looking. It's not enough that

I might not make it out of this woods, but now I can't help thinking: this was inevitable. I had steered my life here.

Getting stuck in a tree with a bear at your feet doesn't happen to people who plan. This was the consequence of letting your life blow around like a leaf.

Lost in life. Now lost in the woods.

But something changed in that tree. Forced to sit long enough to think about my place in the world, I began to ask myself what I wanted from my life — something I had never done before.

A bear or my future. I really didn't know which was scarier.

The journey to this tree began months earlier; that year, four amazing friends tree-planted all summer together. Starting in Ontario, as each contract ended we'd move further west looking for more work, hoping to chase the warmer weather as long as we could. After killing ourselves working all summer, we decided on the ultimate reward for a pack of hormonal and dirty planters: Banff.

We stood along the Trans-Canada Highway with our thumbs out — glaciers and mountains as our backdrop. Finally a car of Aussie tourists picked us up. We drank, danced and partied for a week, before breaking up the pack and going back to school; on our final day we ate magic mushrooms before a long hike up Sulphur Mountain. What should have taken a few hours turned into an entire day, as we kept stopping to giggle at one another. Coming over the crest of the peak, Japanese tourists began snapping photos. *"Famous planters overcome death-defying odds to reach peak."* It snapped us back to reality. Eating ice cream on a patio picnic table, we didn't say much. Just coming off the high and taking it all in. The girls were going back to school in the east; and for the first time in my life, autumn didn't mean school: I had already graduated. So, with most of my belongings in a hockey bag and no place to call home, I kissed my girls goodbye and boarded a Greyhound bus in the opposite direction.

Arriving in Vancouver's Eastside, I planned to see my brother on Hornby Island before starting a new contract in Lillooet, a small logging town north of Whistler. My brother's directions were cryptic: find the boat to Vancouver Island; take another bus about halfway up the island; buy your ferry ticket to Denman Island at the corner store on the highway; "ask the driver where to get off. Don't go into Courtney." And, "while on the Denman Ferry, ask drivers for a lift across Denman — the ferry to Hornby is on the other side of the island. Once on Hornby, I'll meet you at the wharf."

I hadn't seen Michael in about 10 years; when our

parents divorced, he chose to live with my mother in Nova Scotia while I headed in the opposite direction, to Vancouver, with Dad. Eventually he cut himself off from both parents, and much of the world, moved to a remote island and married a woman named Sunshine. But as the ferry pulled into the dock, he was there, or a strange version of him: sunken shoulders, grey hair, and skinny. My first thought: I didn't want to get stuck here. "Michael!" we embraced quickly and deeply.

"I go by Nathan now," he corrects me. This is his middle name. He's also dropped my dad's surname and taken his wife's. I couldn't bring myself to call him Nathan. Growing up, he was Michael — even if he didn't resemble the guy in front of me; he was still Michael to me.

But time had really changed the brother I grew up with. Working odd jobs, he woke whenever he wanted and smoked weed most of the day. "Don't worry so much, Melanie. You're on Hornby time now." That's what I was afraid of: a vortex. Coming from waking up at 5:30 a.m. to plant trees, I craved structure, and purpose. We'd smoke up after coffee and play scrabble most of the day.

A week turned into a month.

"What are you doing there?" It was my mom's best friend back in Ontario, on the phone, checking up on me.

"Don't get lost out there."

Too late. Or was it? Every day I began taking my bike out, at first on the road, then for hour rides along the spectacular cliffside paths, and through meadows that opened out onto the ocean. Returning sweaty and strong, I was hooked. Biking had power.

Not long after being on the island, and feeling that I needed my own space, I bought a beat-up white Chevy cargo van. It was a hunk of a vehicle, with only two seats in the front and nothing in the back, but soon it was filled up with my stuffed animals and a bed frame made from some old two-by-fours. By most standards it wasn't much, but every time I closed the doors and put a cassette into the tape player, I felt secure.

The following week, wedging my bike beside the bed of my new home, I drove off Hornby Island. It was time to work. Even if that meant sawing branches off a tree all day as a tree pruner, it wasn't playing Scrabble.

This was a smaller group than my usual Ontario summer crowd. And like me, they weren't returning to school. We were all in our mid- to late 20s. One guy, with full facial hair and wearing the same plaid shirt every day, was what we called a lifer. He did this full time, all year round. I was scared of being a lifer. Imagine sticking a shovel into the earth vertically and hauling yourself up. By day three of climbing the mountains, imagine your hamstrings as frayed guitar strings ready to snap. But the real clincher: the unrelenting rain that smashed down onto your raw red frozen cheeks.

If there was a mathematical formula to a bad day, this was it; and what's more, every day was the same. Six of them in a row. Oh, did I mention that for miles, not a person in sight? Cry if you want, but it doesn't matter — there's no one around to comfort you. Depression was unavoidable and so began the voices in my head: "You suck, I can't believe you have a degree and you're planting trees for a living." Every day I heard those voices.

But finally, it was here — day six. The day when everything changed for me.

The ordeal started as a bike ride in the woods. And just as it had been on Hornby Island, riding was my escape from people and the monotony of planting. It made me feel different. Anxious to get on the saddle, I didn't even turn back to grab my helmet — I just went. And forget about cell phones; this was 1997.

Rolling past a log cabin, the morning steam is lifting off the lake in front of the mountain. The dirt road veers into a forest so large you could walk for days and never reach the end. Inhaling pine air, pedaling at a steady rhythm, my bike absorbed the bumps. I was floating and free again.

It was hours of blissful smooth meditative pedaling; and somehow, up here, the voices stopped. I felt assured, strong. Capable. Putting my feet down onto the peak, spread out before me was a 360-degree panorama of mountains and forest. And, not a single sound except for my heart and breath. "I will have this moment for the rest of my life. This is mine." And with that, I was ready to begin the fast descent down the other side of the mountain and ready to tackle another dreaded week of planting.

Cool sweat turned to a cold chill on my skin as the bike went faster. Thinking of a warm shower, beer, warm clothes, I let the brakes go completely. "Maybe I'll make some cookies for the guys, maybe I will..." Just then the bike rolled over a dip in the road. I grabbed both brakes with full force, the bike stopped moving, but I didn't. I was launched through the air — up and over the handlebars, over the front tire, and came down onto the road with a thud.

Lifting my head, I couldn't see anything. Darkness.

Slowly the edges of the trees take shape. Touching my head, a handful of hair fell into my palm. Gravel was stuck to the raw flesh on my shoulder and knee; the deep cut on my knee bubbled with burgundy blood. My shoulder felt loose. Running my fingers along my collarbone, the bone jutted out without breaking the skin. Pulling my hand away like I touched a hot stove, I cried. My first broken bone; my body had failed me.

I reached down to pull the bike off to the side of the road, grabbing my ribs to steady my collarbone. I'll come back for it later I think. Lifting my head up, prepared to walk on the road out of the woods, I see it. Staring at me, it's a bear. On the road, maybe 15 metres ahead, it was looking intently at me.

I had to make a move, but how? My arms were glued to my sides. Legs rooted to the road. And all the while, our gaze didn't falter. Maybe it was a concussion or fear, but the forest began to swirl around me. Spinning and spinning faster and faster. And, the only way out of this was to keep walking on the road, past the bear, and that wasn't going to happen. This called for creativity; I decided to bushwhack through the forest in hopes that I could hook up on the road below. Trekking over and under an obstacle of fallen trees, eventually I see a road. Feeling safe walking on the gravel road, I start to think this might be the end of this stupid fucking day. I must be half way down the mountain now. Maybe I'm close to the cabin? I started to think about what I'd do after I got back: *"Oh a bath. I also can't wait to tell this crazy ass story to everyone. Picture it: a room full of people, all eyes on me, glued to my words.*

An hour had passed since my accident and the blood on my knee and shoulder were congealed with bits of gravel. And as I'm thinking this, I look up to see the bear. The same bear. We stop; the surreal swirling trees started again. Considering he's been hibernating all winter, he's most likely hungry. Was it naïve or narcissistic to think this bear wouldn't eat me? I broke a bone today and I never thought that was possible. Was this really something that could happen?

This time it was the bear that retreated into the woods. Is he teasing? Does this mean he's giving me a chance to walk by and then he's going to attack? I keep walking, then running, grabbing onto my shoulder. Looking back, nothing. No bear. Half walking and skipping, I kept moving. Soon we'd be in the dark, just the unpredictable, possibly hungry or limb-tearing, bear and me.

Turning a corner, the switchbacks are getting shorter and I'm getting over excited about being home soon. Around the next bend, something moves on the road. Something brown. But it's too tall for a bear. Three horses. Thank Fuck! These guys will protect me. But as I reach out, my fingertips barely touch its soft hind leg, when the horse shuffles. I move slowly but the pack starts to scamper off. *I call out: Oh no, please stay.* Dropping to my knees, I cried as the dust settles on my wet cheeks. *Come back. Don't leave me alone.*

Slumped into a ball on the road, feeling sorry for myself, this is no way to be. *Get up. Get up.* I slowly lifted my head, and take a few sips of water from my tube attached to my backpack — it's almost empty; my lips are crusty, dry. As I finally get to my feet, it seems like a mirage, but it isn't: the bear. *Go! Go!* Half screaming and crying, I'm screwed. What else can I do?

Backing up, I step off the road into the forest and pick a tree to climb. With my good arm, I chin up to the first branch, and wrap my legs around the branch. I hoist myself up the tree until I reach as far as I can go. Standing on a branch, I can see the sun going down over the trees. Stars eventually appear. And I can see by the green glow of my watch, it's 9:00 p.m. All was quiet in these woods — no wind, or animals. Nothing. But as the adrenalin began to wear off, pain kicks in and intense hunger. Exhaustion. Dropping my forehead onto the tree, I let ants walk over my face.

I was even too tired to think, but I can't help but ruminate about what all of this means. A broken collarbone meant my planting career was over; it would take weeks to heal. I can't afford to wait around. *What if* I move back to Ontario? And leave the mountains? If coming out here taught me one thing, it was that I felt grounded being close to nature, even if my life was chaos. The questions had no answers.

And then, one thing became clear. This story was just another crazy part of my narrative. Despite the broken bones, and fear, I had a story to tell. As weird as it sounds, this adventure was what made me, me, and I wanted to write about it. I wanted to travel the world and have more.

Before getting sucked into my thoughts too deeply, a branch snaps below me, then another. Jesus murphy, what is up with this bear? Four times in one day? The sound stops. Did I imagine it? Thinking back to our first meeting hours ago, it wasn't the biggest bear I had ever seen — like a grizzly that stands on its hind legs, stretching its jaws wide and roaring. But I was baffled by its persistence.

Laying my forehead back on the tree, I'm fading. My body goes limp, and then suddenly snaps to attention before I fall back. I bet everyone is getting ready for the workday tomorrow — laying out the bags, boots, rain gear, having a beer.

It's 11:30. Maybe everyone just went to bed and forgot about me. Maybe they assumed I'm sleeping in my van? It's my fault I didn't tell them where I was going anyway. Then I hear something foreign — a mechanical sound. An engine? It's got to be a car. Oh god, please please. I readjust my legs — bark is digging into my thighs. The engine is getting louder. It is them, it is them. Jesus murphy. But as the engine approaches, and they don't hear my screams, I panic. *"I'm here. I'm here!"* Screaming louder. Oh God, they're going to go past me. Panic spurs an idea. The headlights are shining on my tree. I take off my shoe and as the truck drives beside the tree, I toss it. It lands with a thud on the windshield. The truck stops. "Melanie?" 'Yes, yes! I'm up here!'

That night we drive to Lillooet hospital. I have never been more awake and my body feels every bump in the road; the aches on my cuts, stomach, a headache from dehydration. Holding on to the shower wall with my good arm, a nurse hoses me down. Globs of blood, gravel and sweat swirl down the drain. After tucking me into white sheets, the nurse hands me a bowl of vanilla ice cream, and then I slept for a long time.

Not long after recovering in Whistler for a few weeks, I returned to Ontario with a plan: by September of that same year, I'm in journalism school in Toronto writing. It's not to say that if I wasn't stalked by a bear and held hostage in a tree, I would have become a tree-planting lifer, but I like to think it helped. And not long after graduating, I would begin my life plan: to see as many countries, have as many adventures as possible, on my bike.

A True Canadian Sunset

By Nancy Loucks-McSloy

Growing up with the golden sands of Sauble Beach not far from my doorstep, I didn't realize how rich we really were. Fondly referred to as the "Daytona of Canada," Sauble Beach, Ontario is famous for its 11 kilometres of pure, golden, sugary sand that embrace the warm, clean waters of Lake Huron. Not only is it a spectacular sandy beach, but it has something that is exclusive to Canada — the Lake Huron sunset! The United States, specifically Michigan, has the sunrise over Lake Huron; our shores are blessed with the sunset.

When I visited my relatives in the "city," I envied their beautiful houses, their stylish clothes and even the cookies that came out of a bag instead of the oven. As I take a nostalgic look at the past I now know that what we had, money could not buy. Sure, my cousins had the museums, the malls, the amusement parks and the swimming pools, but they did not have a beach with a sunset.

We lived on a modest farm on Silver Lake Road, just a mile or so from the beach. My parents had grown up during the Great Depression, so frugality was a way of life. On the other hand, they were very generous and giving. My dad would plant a huge garden to feed us throughout the winter and there was always enough for the city relatives who came to visit and take their share of fresh vegetables home with them.

We seldom went out for a fancy dinner or to a movie, but from the time the weather turned nice in the spring, until the snow came and the lake froze over for the winter, we went to the beach. My father always said "Never miss a sunset." In the early spring we would sit at the beach watching the breaking ice formations as they moved in and out and, of course, waiting for that beautiful sunset. As spring turned into summer, we would go to the beach and swim until dusk and then wait to watch the sunset. Summer would turn to autumn, the evenings became chilly and the water would begin to get rough. As we watched the waves, listening to them hit the shore, we would wait for those last sunsets of the season, knowing that soon it would be winter and we would be waiting for spring to once again watch the sunset over the lake. The path to the beach was impassible during the winter, otherwise we would have watched the sunsets year round.

I grew up, married and moved away from the beauty

of the lake and the breathtaking splendour of the sunsets. My parents retired, and looked forward to summer when our children would spend vacations with them. Our children are now grown, with children of their own, but they still talk about the days when Grandma and Grandpa would take them to the beach to swim and how Grandpa always said "Never miss a sunset."

During his golden years Dad would spend his time in the spring puttering around, making maple syrup and preparing to plant his garden. He would come back from the sugar bush in time for dinner and to take that short drive to watch the sunset. During the summer he would work in his garden or relax under the beautiful twin maple trees in the side yard. Evening would come and he would say to Mom, "We better go for an ice cream cone and eat it while we watch the sunset." Autumn was no exception. He still took that short jaunt to the lakeshore most evenings.

Dad had lived on the farm from birth; the only time he had been away from home was during WWII when he was in the army. He always said "There is no place like home, and we have the best – the family farm with a beach at our doorstep."

It was early spring when Dad called with some urgency in his voice, asking us to come and visit for the weekend. A few hours later we were on our way to the farm to spend the weekend helping to make maple syrup. We returned from the sugar bush late in the day with Dad saying, "We better go for a drive, the sunset should be perfect tonight." That was the last sunset that I watched with him.

A week later, we got the shocking call. Just the night before, he and Mom had gone to the beach and watched their last sunset together. Suddenly, he was called to another home. The news was devastating and our next trip home was for his funeral. Spending the next several days at the farm, grieving and not knowing what to do with myself, I would wake up early, drive to the beach, watching and listening to the waves. I felt as if Dad were with me. Every evening, I would say to my family, "if Dad were here he would say 'never miss a sunset,' " and off we would go to watch some of the most spectacular, natural artwork, while reminiscing about a wonderful husband, father and grandpa.

The memories of the sunsets of the Lake Huron shores have never left my heart. No matter what season I am traveling in the area, I feel an urge to be at the beach to view another stunning sunset. The peacefulness and spiritual healing that I have experienced just sitting on the beach watching the sunset is greater therapy for me than money could buy. Living in our crazy, rat race world I have learned to take time to stop and smell the roses. And to never miss a sunset.

WILD SIDE

BY REBECCA ST. PIERRE

I knew they lived nearby. The primal a cappella of eerie, plaintive howls and yips pierced the night air with a chilling, mesmerizing, and yet beautiful cacophony. As one last lone yelp slowly faded away, a pregnant pause was suddenly interrupted by scattered barks from the coyote's domestic cousins. The North American "song" dog, or eastern coyote, had left its mark on the night, warning anyone within hearing distance that it has moved into the area. In hindsight, our meeting was inevitable.

Canada's intimate connection to nature is primarily responsible for my deep admiration and protective embrace of wildlife. As a child camping with my family in Algonquin Park, I discovered that forests, birds, and wild animals offered a world of unrivalled beauty, joy and contentment.

Now, many years later, "home" is a small piece of land on the outskirts of a Canadian city where I can easily access both urban and natural amenities. Downtown London, Ontario, is a mere 15 minute drive away, while a community park and an environmentally significant area (ESA) are within a five-minute walk of my front door. To the west, a new development of houses continues to expand along the southern border of a farmer's field usually sown with corn. As I raise the bedroom blinds each morning, a majestic stand of elderly trees interrupts the northern sky. Squeals of delighted children waft through the air from a city park directly to the east.

The shortened daylight hours of fall always catch me by surprise. Dusk was about an hour away and I needed to take a break from an afternoon spent staring at a computer screen. I sprinted out the door, leaving my SLR camera behind in the rush to enjoy a walk in the waning hours of light. It was a quiet evening. Our neighbours were probably preparing or enjoying dinner, winding down from a day at work, or sharing stories of what they learned at school. I quickly crossed the street and started down a paved section of the meandering Thames Valley Trail through a glorious, small forest.

Recently reborn following the removal of invasive plant species, the wooded area is home to rabbits, cardinals, chipmunks, chickadees, squirrels and a host of other wild animals and birds. Wildlife feed and flourish as Londoners enjoy an afternoon stroll. It is where I sprained an ankle when startled by an overly-friendly fledgling, and encountered my first glimpse of the face behind those haunting night calls.

The October light filtered through the golden and red leaves that still remained on the oak and maple trees. On the left, the short stubble of harvested corn glowed in the fading daylight; on the right, bare limbs of elderly trees reached for drifting clouds. Glimpses of two-storey houses could be seen through the forest scenery. The musky scent of decaying leaves and the chirps of overwintering birds filled the air. I slowed my pace.

The farmer's field bordering the forest is a daily, surprise medley of wildlife. It had been painted black with a flock of approximately 20 wild turkeys earlier in the summer. Skittish birds, they seemed to sense they were being watched, and with amazing speed silently disappeared into a large forest on the opposite side of the field. Deer also graze in the area. With a quick flick of their white tails, somewhat resembling a rude farewell gesture, they escape from sight in surprisingly high leaps and bounds. On one occasion I came within two metres of a fawn as it stopped to nibble on the tender shoots of a tree bordering the field. One day a great blue heron decided to look for lunch, not at the nearby pond, but in the stubble of corn stalks.

As I walked I glanced to my left periodically to check for any signs of large wildlife. And that is when I saw it prancing through the corn stubble, about a hundred metres away, heading in the opposite direction, towards the street I had just crossed, the new housing development, and my home. The silhouette did not resemble a deer, or turkey, or heron as it zigzagged across the open field with graceful agility and speed. It did not appear frightened or hurried. Head down, it was focused on one goal: food. Since my zoom lens and binoculars were back at home, I reached for my cell phone camera. A few quick clicks and a magnified photo revealed a dog or dog-like mammal. It appeared to be looking over its shoulder at me in one shot. I looked up; it was nowhere in sight. I had just seen my first coyote.

Stories circulated of people seeing coyotes while hiking with their dogs – apparently small dogs are a coyote magnet – and City of London signs appeared at path entrances warning hikers to be watchful for coyotes at dawn and dusk. But it was a photograph of an adult coyote taking an afternoon siesta in a neighbour's backyard that had started my fingers flying across the keyboard three weeks earlier to learn more about these creatures. That neighbour lived just a two-minute jaunt down the road.

Thanks to Google, I learned coyotes are curious, intelligent, non-confrontational creatures. Their opportunistic behaviour makes them perfectly suited to thriving in the urban environment. Retracing my steps in the hope of catching a glimpse of the wild animal proved to be fruitless. I slowly resumed my walk, stopping frequently to glance over my shoulder.

The forested section of this path transitions into an open area with a stormwater pond. Typically, the resident great blue heron patiently waits for his next meal at the water's edge, and the local belted kingfisher's raucous call fills the air as he flies back and forth between two water level gauges. Canada geese and mallards peacefully coexist on the narrow strip of land dividing the pond in half. Parades of ducklings frantically paddle behind their parent, with invariably one struggling to keep up with its siblings. Bald eagles sometimes grace the sky with a splendid soaring dance on cloudless days. Occasionally disputes arise, like the day an elegant great egret regretfully challenged the great blue heron's territory. No sign of the coyote.

The path bridges nature and mankind with fenced backyards on one side and a 28-hectare mature forest on the other. Juvenile eastern cottontails graze at the path's edge in late summer, and herds of white-tailed deer feast on fresh grain spread near the backyard fencing in the dead of winter. As the sun sank lower on the horizon, I hurried past a group of houses under construction, crossed the street and entered a park. Home was less than five minutes away.

Our community park has evolved over the past seven years, since we moved into the area. Visitors can stroll along one of several paths, relax on a bench, or find shelter under one of two mature trees. During the summer months young children chase each other around the playground swing sets, as youth enjoy the basketball courts, and supportive family and friends cheer on youngsters playing soccer or baseball. One section of the park remains wild to protect the species-at-risk bobolink that nests in the area. Perhaps today would be the day when I finally caught a glimpse of the striking black, white, and yellow bird.

The only other person in the park was engrossed in a cell phone conversation while her dog sniffed at a particularly interesting patch of grass. As a canine barked incessantly from across the street and birds flitted between newly planted saplings, a coyote appeared in the baseball diamond outfield. It headed directly for the tall grass, the woman, and her dog. And that was when I realized her pet was not on a leash. One other valuable tip I had learned online: coyotes may attack unattended dogs.

Time paused. If I screamed, the woman would see the coyote, but the coyote would then notice the dog. Dashing across the park to warn her also posed problems; running attracts a coyote's attention. What canine doesn't enjoy a game of chase? The coyote and I were now an equal distance from them.

Frantic waving arms and exaggerated pointing in the direction of the wild animal finally grabbed the woman's attention. Over the next few seconds, her look of annoyance transformed into confusion, and finally fear, as she slowly turned around 180 degrees to face the coyote, her cell phone still firmly sandwiched between head and hand. The coyote pounced in the tall grass seemingly oblivious to everything but the tasty morsel it was trying to coax out of hiding.

Time accelerated. Realizing her pet could be in danger, the woman lunged to grab its collar. The dog dashed to the right, then the left. Focused on the joy of freedom and playing, it did not see its wild cousin 15 metres away. Five minutes later, the woman mouthed a silent "thank you" as she briskly exited the park with her leashed dog. I stayed behind.

Dusk's warm light softened the coyote's features as it raised its handsome head to look over the terrain. As I peered through the wire fencing of the baseball diamond's backstop I could see how it resembled a German shepherd. Streamlined and yet muscular, the coyote was the athletic version of its cousin, the domestic dog. This looked to be one healthy, well-fed wild animal. The coyote's physique screamed endurance and speed from its tan and white pointed muzzle, to the large triangular ears, across its dark haunches to the tip of the coyote's bushy tail. I dug my cell phone out of my pocket without taking my eyes off the wild animal and called my husband. We lived three houses away. I had barely pocketed the phone when he appeared with our camera.

Photo by Rebecca St. Pierre

Coyotes and wolves have bred over the years to produce a hybrid, sometimes referred to as a "coywolf". If my memory served me correctly, I was staring at a perfect example of this genetic mingling. The coyote looked at my husband, a tall man who is not easily missed. It turned away after a quick assessment and returned to ridding the neighbourhood of rodents. My husband and I nodded to one another in agreement that the coyote's dismissal was our cue to return home where, in the months that followed, I had a new appreciation for the hauntingly beautiful voices of our neighbouring wild canines.

CELEBRATION OF LIGHT

BY CATHERINE COCCHIO

All the smoke and thundering explosions of colour showering from the sky in any fireworks or laser light display I've ever seen will never match the natural celebration of light our family witnessed one night while travelling home from an early season out-of-town hockey game.

On an otherwise stark and lonely stretch of highway in Southwestern Ontario an unusual light in the sky caught my eye as I turned to hand a snack to my son in the back seat of the car. Too late to attribute the sight to lingering reflections of sunset, I studied the shifting patterns of blue, green, and white light oscillating in various patterns, smearing wisps of brilliant colour across the black sky.

Not sure I should trust my weary eyes, I enlisted the help of our son's sharp night vision to confirm my observations. Doing his teenaged best to recall a recent science lesson, he recounted how the interaction of electricity and gases in the air sometimes cause a phenomenon known as the northern lights.

As improbable as it seemed so far south in Canada, we guessed that must account for what appeared before us in the northern sky. Waiting for a safe break in traffic, my husband pulled the car off to the side of the road for a better look.

Like frosted bands of colour shredded from a rainbow and strewn recklessly in shards of shooting light, they painted the sky. Swimming majestically from pattern to pattern, the light show needed no music or commentary to hold our attention.

The sky reminded me of a story I'd read in school in which Olga, a young Norwegian girl, told of watching bright yellow, pink, and white colours dancing like fairies in the winter sky. I remembered wishing I too would one day see their magnificence. Mesmerized by the power of the display, I understood the value of believing that wishes really do come true.

Pushed by the advancing hour we returned reluctantly to the car, and continued on our way. The light show followed us until it disappeared, swallowed up by the bright glow of the city sky.

Early the next morning, I hurried down to the basement in search of the book with the story of the little Norwegian girl and her fabulous colours. Happily, it was still there, but oddly enough, not exactly as I remembered.

To my amazement, the story and illustration that had painted such vivid pictures of Olga and her northern lights appeared in stark black and white.

The imagination of a child had coloured those powerful images of the past. Our experience last night lifted them from the page, to finally colour the picture real.

Photo by Sheila Creighton

PLANTING HOPE

BY SHEILA CREIGHTON

Riley looked toward me, exuding the sheer joy of a not quite jaded nine-year-old. He hung on every word Tom said. It was then I knew that this day had changed his life. A brilliant light had been turned on as he looked up through the bold leaves of a tulip tree to the cloudless sky.

"We need a name for this project," Julie, my colleague, said as she swung around in her chair and faced me. "How about Growing Community or Greening Lives?" I responded, knowing how important it was to her that this project connect people through planting trees. "Planting Hope?"

Julie suggested. "That's good," I said "although maybe a bit cheesy." We laughed. It is not always an easy task to put words to emotions and actions. It had been a new idea for us to go into a housing project and add some much needed natural energy and human caring.

Impact, we're always measuring impact. But how does one illustrate the impact of trees on people and their state of mind? Environmental impact is easy but who does our work affect, and does the effect last? Can we change behaviour and make connections that can help the future? This particular project, focused on impacting people's lives directly, began with a successful grant application, a landscape architect's plan, and caring individuals who walk the walk of building community in the lives of people living in low-income situations. Julie was one of these people who had this vision and was hoping to see it fulfilled.

The warm day in May finally arrived for the planting project, in what some people might also refer to as a project – a housing complex of low-income families, with 30 per cent of them children under 16, and over 30 different languages spoken. These are decent people scraping by to provide for their families, living day-to-day without much light breaking through the cracks.

I arrived early armed with my camera and photo

release forms, prepared for another routine event taking pictures of smiling people planting trees. Ahead of time I had thought it would be the same as other plantings, but I felt right away this was going to be different. It was either going to be a huge success or a huge disaster. I was not sure which, so I had an overwhelming feeling of uneasiness joined with intense energy.

Fifteen or so children were already there, most seven to 10 years of age. There were a few moms cautiously keeping an eye on things from various vantage points. The kids watched excitedly as equipment and trees were unloaded. A huge pile of mulch sat off to one side providing an amazing 'king of the mountain' location that a few of the boys took advantage of, laughing loudly as they slid down the side of it. Girls were drawing hearts and stars in chalk all along the sidewalk, giggling. These young people were all residents but I could tell that most did not know each other. As they surveyed the task at hand and formed groups to start digging, I could see new friendships developing.

Julie took a microphone and welcomed everyone to the planting. "Thank you for being part of this exciting project," she said to the group as the animated chatter lulled. "We know today will be a lot of fun. Trees are part of what makes a house a home and this new space will be a gathering place to build a stronger community for you, a place you can enjoy and get to know your neighbours."

People were dressed in colourful shorts and t-shirts. It felt like summer. The scents of fresh earth, pine mulch and coconut sunscreen permeated the air. A local radio station joined us for a live remote, playing pop and rock music with an infectious beat to work along to, with some people even singing along. It was a festive atmosphere.

The site was an open common area that needed some attention. An attractive landscape design had been professionally prepared, and centred on the sole existing tree. Ten large pieces of Armour Stone, seating for this installation, had been set in place ahead of time. The task at hand was to plant five 10 to 15 foot trees native to London, Ontario and the Carolinian Zone. Hardy Canadian trees for our climate. They were to be spaced along a wavy line, and 18 native shrubs would be planted to fill in between the trees. The whole thing would need pine mulch around it to give it that finished landscape look. It's a technique that works well and fills in fast, creating a nice leafy green space.

I made sure that I had as many signed photo releases as I could get before the action started. As parents had to sign these releases, and most were not in attendance, each child ran home with his or her form. Most came running back smiling and waving their signed permission forms, but a few wandered slowly back to me with their heads hanging down, saying their mom had said no.

"That's okay," I said, "I can always photograph your feet or hands or even this amazing chalk art you did!" I said to one little girl, who seemed pleased that I knew which artwork was hers.

As a photographer documenting an event, I find it easier to follow a few people in a group and work at getting some good images of them. I chose to focus on a group of three young boys, Riley, Jamal, and Luke. They were around nine years of age, still young enough to be excited by the possibilities.

These three were happy to pose and did the usual silly things young boys do when they're suddenly in the spotlight. Riley played it cool and showed off his bicep. Jamal made some hand gestures and tried to look tough. Luke shyly joined the other two, pulling a funny face. They did not know each other but they quickly formed a bond to get two large holes dug in the most efficient way. All three were diligent and determined.

As the children worked at getting the holes dug, the shrubs in place, and the mulch ready, others gradually came out to see what was going on. What started as only a few parents soon became many moms and a few dads, joining in or sitting on the sidelines, meeting their neighbours, pointing out their children to each other, and letting their respective guards down. One mom who had earlier refused to sign a photo release asked me for one so her son and daughter could have their photo taken too. One dad joined his daughters in planting a clump of white birch, to the visible delight of the girls who had thrown caution to the wind and were getting covered in dirt.

Tom, who grows these native trees, was on hand with his staff to help install them. When the holes were ready, he carefully brought each heavy tree over to be planted. He showed the kids how to ready the hole for planting, take off any root ball ties, and how, together, to set the large trees into their new home. Riley asked so many questions. "How do you know the hole is deep enough? What kind of tree is this? How big will it get? Why is it called a tulip tree? How much water does it need? Is this your job?" Tom smiled widely and happily answered each question in detail. Riley beamed as Tom answered him.

"You could be a landscape designer or an arborist or even grow trees," I said to Riley. He nodded in a thoughtful way, his face filled with happiness as he studied the tulip tree's unusual leaves.

The hose, that was never allowed to be turned on, and that we knew had been shut off by the complex due to misuse by kids, suddenly flowed with clear, fresh water. Riley, Jamal and Luke sprayed each other, laughing heartily while they filled buckets for watering the new trees. Kids lined up to fill their buckets, enjoying the cooling spray. The atmosphere of accomplishment and camaraderie was as welcome as the smell of barbecued hot dogs.

As the planting was nearing completion, Julie again took to the mic. "Thank you for all your hard work making this green outdoor space a reality! I hope you all sign up to take care of these trees and shrubs." A woman from the complex held up a clipboard. "There's a schedule for watering and they will need a lot of water for the first few years, especially this summer," Julie continued. "They're your trees and we need you to take care of them. Now for a job well done, we're going to be serving hot dogs and ice cream." Cheers and applause broke out, and then attention switched to lunch.

A tough looking teenage boy, attracted by the music, stood a short distance away from the activity, mumbling under his breath. Julie approached him and encouraged him to join in. "Nah, they're all going to get trashed," he said. "Well you can help make sure they don't," Julie said without hesitation. After a moment he said, "Yeah, I guess. My brother sure seems happy about it." Julie smiled. "Come and have a hot dog and some ice cream." Her direct approach must have worked because a few minutes later he sauntered over, got a hot dog and sat down on the rocks to check out the new hangout.

As the team gathered up the equipment and started loading up the trucks, the ice cream sandwiches were given out. It became apparent that we had ordered far too much ice cream, so each child who had helped was offered a full box of ice cream sandwiches to take home. I'll never forget the sight of a young boy running home squealing with joy with a box of ice cream sandwiches hoisted above his head like he was carrying the Stanley Cup.

I stood off to the side for a while just watching and thinking. Although I knew that research studies show trees build community, before this day it had not resonated with me; it was only written in studies done in other places. Today, trees had made an impact on the lives of these people. Later we would hear some amazing feedback from residents. One woman told us she had made new friends that day and was no longer afraid of her neighbours. Another woman told us about her son, an uninterested, struggling reader, who started going out to the 'reading rocks' every evening.

A housing complex can be vibrant, green and full of positive energy. This planting sparked something in Riley, and likely several others. I know these kids will take ownership of this leafy gathering area and will visit this spot for many years to come to see how big their trees have grown.

After everything was packed up and ready to go, Julie and I stood and surveyed a most attractive landscaped area. I knew how much she had wanted this to be the success it was. I felt grateful for her vision, knowing I would never forget this day. I turned to her and said, "Planting Hope… guess it's not such a cheesy name after all."

OTHER
TRUE
TALES

TIME TRAVEL

BY EVELYN SYMONS

I am easily distracted, as one train of thought pulls into the station and another pulls out. I'm on a self-imposed journey to attach a parcel of descriptive words and feelings to nearly 10 million square kilometres – Canada.

As a photographer, I have experienced the magnificence of our landscapes, and I confess to being emotional when surrounded by nature's inspiring artwork. I've had to step away from the camera to wipe my eyes more than a few times. As a journalist, I have interviewed hundreds of people, from those attending a Canada Day celebration for their first time to those who share the traditions of their ancestors. Passion is the common thread woven through each story.

I walk the woods behind my Southwestern Ontario home to clear my mind. My attention goes to a deer. She stands quietly among the trees on the ridge above the bog that surrounds a glacial kettle pond. My dog notices me looking up. He sees her too. He barks once and she's gone.

The leaves of the American Beech trees rustle in

the breeze even though it's January. Many of the light tan-coloured leaves stay on the trees until the spring sets forth new tender green foliage. I step over fallen trees that are alive in new ways. Their sap no longer flows, and they are home to moss, insects and fungus. They offer a secure hiding place for snakes and salamanders in the boggy environment.

I sit down on a granite rock to think about my question. What is Canada to me? How can I possibly describe it? It's easy to feel the essence of the woods as it surrounds me, but how do I expand that feeling to include all of Canada? While I rest in the understory of the trees I think back to when I too was protected by the tall and strong.

I've always been attracted to nature. Each time my family moved when I was a child, we were never far from a green space. The first time I found myself in a city, I wandered the fields of Elgin Mills in Richmond Hill. I played in the orchard that was, at the time, at the end of Neil Drive where my school, Beverley Acres, stood and still stands. It seemed so easy to be a kid in the '60s.

As the fall turned into winter, our anticipation of enjoying the school's annual skating rink grew. We kept our eyes on the custodian. We'd gather around him. We'd ask him when the boards would be going up, but he did not entertain our questions. He kept his secret and his steely demeanor. When the boards finally went up, the surface flooded and frozen, students rushed to school, skates slung over their shoulders.

We had a designated snowball throwing area on the parimeter of the grounds. Teaming up, one kid would make the snowballs and put them in the hood of their winter coat. This gave the advantage to the one who was throwing. Then we switched roles so everyone had a chance to show off their pitching arm, with snowballs flying in complete disorder. The amount of fun was measured by the number of wet woolen mittens lying across the classroom heat vents, in hopes they would dry before we headed back out to play.

When the Christmas season arrived, our teachers corralled the entire student body into the hallways. Our instructions were to sit on the floor in rows. Teachers handed out Christmas carol sheets. What was about to happen should have been an Olympic sport, what with the patience, attention and timing required of all the staff. The energy of hundreds of students bounced off the walls; even the teachers were giddy.

The school fell mostly silent as we tuned into the teachers' signals: the nods, the shaking of heads and the nearly-there smiles. Every class had to be ready. The attention was not unlike the Academy of St Martin in the Fields watching Neville Marriner, save for the running noses and odd socks of the cross-legged choir, rather than a fine orchestra. Finally the moment came. The hands of the teacher carved the air with up and downward motions as she conducted us to begin singing.

Our voices rose as one, the song resonating through the hallways. The timing can only be described as a miracle – a Christmas miracle. I don't remember what carol we started with; it didn't matter as hundreds of small- and medium-sized hands held on tightly to the song sheets, white with green lettering. Our enthusiasm stayed alive even through the words of "Good King Wenceslas."

Bullying was not part of a regular day. I do remember some teasing of a boy named Gary. He had a glass eye. The boys involved quickly realized that their teasing was completely offset by the girls' kind attention to young Gary. If anyone was seen wrestling or fist fighting in the playground, a teacher would meander over, wait for them to tire themselves out and have them shake hands. Bullies don't like to shake hands so fights seldom happened.

It seemed to me we didn't waste our time on sparring. There was fun to be had, baseball to be played, ropes to be jumped, and rubber balls to be tossed against the wall in rhythm – one hand, the other hand, one foot, the other foot.

On the home front, my father was an advertising manager for the country and western radio station CFGM. I had
the chance to meet Tommy Hunter, the singer later described
as "Canada's Country Gentleman." His band performed at
Wilson Niblett Motors, a company that is still in Richmond
Hill 50 years later. Both the band and dealership flourished
from the attention. When "The Tommy Hunter Show" first
aired on CBC in 1965, I felt privileged to have met him.

Timothy Findley, a much-loved Canadian author,
playwright and storyteller, was then a copyright editor at
the radio station. Many years later, my son Jonathan went
to Findley's book reading and signing of *Spadework* in 2001.
The book purchase was a gift for me. He dutifully waited
in line to have the book signed. Jonathan told Findley who
his grandfather was. Sitting next to Findley was his long-
time companion William Whitehead. His comments caught
Jonathan off guard. Calling him a young feller, Whitehead
had no qualms about telling my son that his grandfather had
almost worked Findley to death. If true, Findley seemed to
hold no grudge. Thankfully, the inscription reads "For Evelyn
– With cordial greetings."

I left that school in Grade 5, with memories of having
been one of the only children in kindergarten to know my
full address and telephone number, and how to spell my last

name. No one deliberately taught me. I heard my mother ordering items over the phone from the Eaton's and Simpson's catalogues – 324 Skopit Road – S-K-O-P-I-T. My mother's soft but firm voice spelled out the letters of our address and last name. I can still recall the phone number.

I stand up from my comfortable rock in the woods, memories from the past mingling with the scenery around me. I can hear the young voices in school as we started each day singing our national anthem, "O Canada". The words glorious and free loop in my mind – glorious and free.

That wasn't as difficult as I thought it would be. I now have the words.

LEGACY OF THE WORN OUT SHOES
A CANADIAN PARTICIPACTION STORY

BY CATHERINE COCCHIO

Not long after my son took his first steps, he figured out that there was a faster, better way to get around. He's been running ever since. As a matter of fact, running was one of the main reasons he obtained an athletic scholarship for university.

Although he crossed many start/finish lines along the way, it turns out races he completed before going away to school actually left behind a greater legacy for me, the driver he depended on for rides to early morning races in the City of Windsor and Essex County.

There was a spirit of fraternity among the participants that set race days apart from regular training days. Competitors seemed to focus on personal accomplishment rather than actual prizes or podium placements. One day, a local sporting goods store donated a pair of spikes to the first to finish. That gave my son an idea. Why should his driver stand around and wait for him at the finish line every race? Wouldn't it be better for her to share the fun?

Since Mother's Day was just around the corner, he decided to surprise me with a new pair of walking shoes with a note inviting me to walk the next 5K while he ran his 10K. After assurances that I would not be the last person to finish, I reluctantly found myself lined up at the front of the pack with an intimidatingly large group of competitors. The starter's gun sounded and the shoes responded, rocking out a steady heel-toe beat down the course.

Huffing and puffing along with walkers chatting about their bypass surgeries and hip replacements, I began to doubt I'd even make it to the half way point when I looked ahead to see my son already on his way back to the finish! His smile gave me all the energy I needed to make sure this time I'd be the one crossing the finish line to his welcoming cheers.

That day, after literally walking a mile (or two) in his shoes, I may not have taken a place on the podium, but I left the race feeling happier than those who had. I won the best prize of all, a totally new understanding of what the runner/walker's life was all about.

Later that season our runner passed his driving test. He no longer needed me to drive him to competition. With all the extra time to myself, I began to walk a daily 5 K route. Every day since then I think, dream, see things differently, and come home feeling refreshed. I have no idea how far I've travelled, but I know I feel wonderful. The original Mother's Day shoes wore out long ago, but their legacy continues to grow every day, one step at a time.

The ParticipACTION program was launched in the 1970s to promote healthy living and physical fitness. It encourages Canadians to sit less and move more, and to make physical activity a vital part of everyday life.

THE SECRET THAT WON THE WAR

BY NICOLE LAIDLER

Sometimes you meet an individual you know you'll remember for the rest of your life. Fred Bates was such a man.

When I interviewed Bates, he was close to the end of his life and living in a modest apartment near Springbank Park. I was a journalism student in search of a source for a class assignment. Bates was about to share a secret that he had lived with for more than 50 years. It was a secret that had changed the course of history, one that he and thousands of other Canadian World War II veterans had sworn to protect. It was the secret of radar.

Today radar is used to catch speeding drivers and treat cancer patients. During the war, it was at the centre of a technological cat-and-mouse race between the Germans and the Allies.

Both sides understood that radar could detect unseen enemy aircraft, battleships, and submarines. It could be used to direct precision bombing raids – even under the cover of darkness. It would play a role in every battle.

More than 6,000 Canadian soldiers were inducted into the Allied radar program. But to the outside world these radar recruits simply did not exist. Their uniforms bore no special insignia. They were forbidden to speak about their work. And when the war was won, they were simply discharged and sent home. Their role in the Allied victory would not be officially recognized for another half-century.

The father of British radar, Sir Robert Watson-Watt, first demonstrated how radio waves could be used to detect far-away objects on February 26, 1935. Using a BBC short-wave radio transmitter, Watt's team sent a beam of electromagnetic radiation out into the atmosphere. The pulse hit an RAF heavy bomber and ricocheted back to earth.

The echo was picked up by a receiver located eight miles away. By timing how long it took the signal to go out and return, the scientists could detect the presence of the plane and pinpoint its location.

When Britain declared war on September 3, 1939, the island country was already protected by an invisible shield of about 20 rudimentary radar stations called Chain Home. By the following spring a new type of radar had been developed.

It could detect low-flying planes over longer distances. By the summer of 1940, more than 70 radar towers stood guard against enemy aircraft.

The RAF's uncanny ability to 'see' and intercept nighttime German bombing raids during the Battle of Britain was not due to a diet rich in carrots, as was widely reported in the press. It was due to the efforts of thousands of highly-trained men and women secretly working at what was now called Chain Home Low.

Struggling to keep the stations operational around the clock, Britain appealed to Commonwealth countries, including Canada, Australia and New Zealand, for help. Canada agreed to send 5,000 men.

Many of Canada's radar veterans took their stories to the grave. But not 121073 Flight Lieutenant G.F. Bates. As the 87-year-old settled into his armchair, his memories came flooding back.

A storekeeper from Wingham, Ontario, Bates travelled to London to enlist in the Royal Canadian Air Force in October 1941. He had no way of knowing that he had just joined a top-secret division of the British Commonwealth's air training program.

Bates was shipped off to school for a crash course in radio and electronics. He joined 120 young men at the

Ontario Agricultural College in Guelph, one of 13 Canadian universities to participate in the program. "They assumed we were already university graduates and knew a little about radio," Bates recalled. With only a high school diploma and no radio background, he found it hard to keep up with the lectures. "I got up and protested," he said. "They took a survey of the class and found that half of us were in the same boat."

After 13 weeks of intensive study, Bates knew enough about the flow of atoms to move on to the next stage of training. Still believing he was preparing for a career as a radio mechanic, he was posted to No. 31 Range and Direction Finding (RDF), Clinton. He was in for a shock.

Britain's first radar officers, mechanics and operators were trained at Yatesbury and Cranwell. Located in southern England, both schools were in easy bombing range of the Germans. The RAF needed to find a more secure location. They chose Tyndell Farm, four miles outside of Clinton, Ontario.

Hidden in the rolling hills of Huron County, just 50 kilometres north of London, the Clinton school would train more than 7,000 radar recruits by the end of the war. With the rugged bluffs of Lake Huron less than 16 kilometres away, the location offered ideal conditions for the British RDF training station.

The school officially opened on July 20, 1941. Bates arrived early the following year. "There was snow on the ground and they were still building the labs and dormitories," he recalled.

Bates joined his classmates in the air force hanger. "We were all lined up. One at a time, they made us swear on the Bible that we wouldn't disclose what we were doing, what the frequency was, or even what it was called. Nothing. Not even from one student to another." Each recruit pledged to maintain their silence for the next 50 years. "They really put the boots to us on that one," said Bates. "So much so that very few of the radar types will even talk about it today."

Extraordinary measures were taken to protect radar's secrets – even in rural Ontario.

The Clinton air base was surrounded by an electrified barbed-wire fence. Classes were held under armed guard inside a separate inner compound. Notebooks and other learning materials were considered classified documents and remained inside the classroom.

Group Captain Adrian Cocks was the commanding officer. "He had a phobia that the Germans were going to bomb his radar station," Bates remembered. A corn silo at the edge of the muddy parade ground was manned with a search light and two armed sentries, just in case.

RAF Clinton was under British control and the Canadian soldiers were fed British rations – powdered milk, Spam, and one egg per week. Food was a major source of discontent, said Bates, especially since the camp was surrounded by farms. "We could hear the cows bellowing away over the back fence and the chickens and roosters crowing in the morning."

By the time the Royal Canadian Air Force brought in chefs from Toronto's Royal York Hotel to quell the unrest, Bates was already in British Columbia installing four of the eight radar stations that would protect Canada's west coast.

"I'd never seen that type of radar before," said Bates, who was now an officer. The equipment was smaller and had a higher frequency than what he had been trained on in Clinton.

The stations replaced coast watchers, pairs of men equipped with a rifle, radio pack and a pair of binoculars. "We were already at war with Japan, and that had been the defense of Canada," Bates said.

Bates installed 28 tons of radar equipment in the remote Queen Charlotte Islands, unofficially recruiting nine coast watchers to help. "There were dozens of cartons, steel frames, and antennas lying all over the soggy, wet ground."

But the secret of radar was kept. Bates never told the men how the equipment worked or what it was for.

Bates was shipped overseas in 1943, joining thousands of other Clinton graduates who would take part in military campaigns throughout Europe, North Africa, Asia and Russia.

Sent to RAF Halkshill Downs in England, Bates would become a technical officer for one of Britain's most carefully-guarded secrets, a highly-sophisticated offensive radar system called Oboe.

Oboe was used to direct England's light-weight Mosquito bombers. The plane's navigator listened for acoustic signals – dots if the plane was off-course in one direction, dashes if in the other. When the plane was on the correct flight path a constant tone was heard. It sounded like an oboe.

Oboe could control a plane's position over a 750-mile range, Bates explained. "From Dover that's down to the Italian Alps, over to Berlin, and to the tip of Norway." From an altitude of 32,000 feet, the British Mosquitoes could release their bombs accurately within a radius of three metres.

Sometimes Oboe was used for friendlier purposes. During the Dutch famine of 1944, the British made Spam raids over several cities, using radar technology to drop food packages onto individual apartment buildings.

Bates' brother, who was working with the Red Cross in Holland, came to England for a visit. "Here was my brother telling me about the food hampers coming down, and what do you think I was doing? I was running Spam raids," said Bates, chuckling. "He was sitting on a blanket on the cliffs outside of Dover yakking away about what we were doing and I – straight faced – couldn't tell him a thing."

Bates was discharged shortly before the end of the war. He returned to London, Ontario, and opened a company designing, producing, and servicing electronic equipment.

The first radar reunion took place in Coventry England in 1991. The British government lifted the vow of secrecy, and for the first time, the World War Two radar veterans could speak openly about their past.

Bates never forgot his wartime experiences. Worried that irreplaceable materials would be lost forever, he formed a committee and got to work. The Secrets of Radar Museum opened on the grounds of London's Parkwood Institute, which has a long history of providing care for veterans, on May 24, 2003. 121073 Flight Lieutenant G.F. Bates spent every Saturday morning giving guided tours of the four-room facility.

Bates passed away on March 8, 2004, less than two weeks after we spoke. I never had the chance to thank him for welcoming me into his home and for trusting me with his wartime memories. This was his story. And it's one I will never forget.

HANS ACROSS THE WATER

BY OTTE ROSENKRANTZ

There are no doubt as many immigrant stories as there are immigrants, but the one thing I believe is true for all of us who are newcomers to Canada is that we never truly leave our home countries behind. In my case that country is Denmark, and although I have lived in Canada for more than 40 years, news about Denmark still feels like news from home. Back in 2005 I felt, in a small way, an ongoing tug-of-war between loyalties. It was the impetus for the following story.

Things were getting hot in the Arctic. Denmark, which claims to own a 1.3 square kilometre hunk of rock called Hans Island between the coast of Greenland and Ellesmere Island in the Nares Strait, sent a warship to the region to protect the island from further incursions by the Canadian military. The fact that there would barely be room on the island for both Canadian and Danish personnel to engage in a rousing game of arm wrestling, much less actual fighting, was of no matter. The Danes claimed the rock as their property, and Canada would be scuppered if it conceded the land without a fight – or at least a good shoving match.

Comparisons were sombrely drawn between the rising tensions around the ownership of Hans Island and the war in the Falklands – also known as the Malvinas – in 1982. But the comparison didn't stand up. For one thing, the Falklands have sheep and grass and houses and people. Hans Island has lichen – and very little lichen at that. For another, the world powers that clashed over the Falklands were England and Argentina, both countries with attitude, and the military might to back that attitude.

The countries locked in a diplomatic spat over an Arctic island that doesn't even have guano on it were Canada and Denmark, countries better known for trying to get the rest of the world to calm down, than for flexing their own military might. Having Canada and Denmark sword-rattling at each other over Hans Island was a bit like having a couple of eighth-graders at computer camp challenging each other to a pillow fight over who gets the top bunk: it really doesn't matter, and the other kids find the posturing funny.

There was, of course, no lack of experts getting up on television to talk about the gravity of this situation, and why we should all stop snickering and take this seriously.

Apparently, and get this, Hans Island is important because when global warming melts all that nasty ice up there and opens up the Northwest passage to commercial activity, whoever owns Hans Island will control the passage – a sort of Gibraltar of the far north, without the monkeys, of course.

What the experts neglected to consider is that, for one thing, Hans is too small to allow either country to build a decent gun emplacement there, and for another, when global warming has melted all that ice, Hans Island, which is barely a rocky bubble over the ice as it is, will be in all likelihood under several feet of water, and Canada and Denmark and all the other countries with people living along shorelines will have other things to worry about, such as how to pump the Atlantic out of their basements.

The Danes and their gunboat were planning to replace a Danish flag which had "fallen over" at about the same time then-Canadian Minister of Defence Graham Bill had himself helicoptered to the Island to place a Canadian flag there – I'm guessing the island was not big enough for both flags.

Of course, Graham was not entirely to blame for igniting that latest round of tiffing over ownership of the island. In 1984, Denmark's minister of Greenland affairs raised a Danish flag on the island. He then buried a bottle of brandy at the base of the flagpole and left a note saying "Welcome to the Danish island." Presumably the bottle was intended as bait to lure Canadian government officials there, and render them incapable of fighting. Perhaps Minister Graham was there in search of ice cubes. Had I known about the bottle earlier, I would have gone myself. Beats paying the markup at the LCBO.

I wondered what the Danes were planning to leave there during this, their latest visit. A large cask of blue cheese and herring? Have those people no sense of decency? And I'm part Danish. Do they not know that the Canadian military is not prepared for such biological warfare?

Meanwhile, tens of people around the globe were holding their collective breath, wondering how it would turn out.

In a world which seems determined to drive itself to madness through violence and greed, we have to be grateful to the Danes and the Canadians for providing a little comic relief during such a long, hot and smoggy Canadian summer. Good for them.

As a proud Canadian of equally proud Danish heritage, I'm still hoping to visit Hans Island before the ice melts. And is the brandy still there? Meanwhile, the National Post reported the following on July 20, 2012:

"In a joint Canada-Denmark corporate pairing, a specially brewed Danish beer called 'Hans Across the Water' arrives this week for a Canada-only release. Featuring a colourful label of a sandy-haired Dane reaching across the ocean to pour a beer for a bespectacled Canadian, its slogan is: 'Make Beer Not War.'"

Skol!

MY STRATFORD DEBUT

BY MARK KEARNEY

I'm a writer, not a dancer.

And yet, in early June 2016, I finally made my debut on the Stratford Festival Theatre stage – not because of my proficiency with the pen but because of my smooth, fluid moves. Okay, I really can't confirm if "smooth" and "fluid" were the actual words the audience was thinking when they saw me in a dance called Running the Goat.

Stratford fans may remember that that year's production of *As You Like It* was set in Newfoundland, and included performances where 16 members of the audience came onstage to dance during the final scene.

So, you may think that old joke – "How do you get to Carnegie Hall? Practise, practise, practise" applies here. You're thinking, poor guy, all those long hours of rehearsals, trying to master the complex choreography, the intricacy of the steps. The countless auditions over the years … suffering rejection after rejection, his spirit battered as he relentlessly pursued the elusive fantasy.

Nahhh.

You show up an hour before the performance and someone in the company walks you through the various dance steps and where you'll be on stage. You do so in groups of four couples and ultimately, onstage, one of those pairs is made up of two of the play's actors who can pretty much adjust to any mistakes you make. And you will make mistakes. It's basically like square dancing, so a big shout out to my high school Phys. Ed. teachers who showed us a few do-si-dos back in the day.

Still, not just anyone could do this. Give me some credit. I had to book my ticket months ahead of the performance night to be part of that magical 16.

Oh, wait, my wife did that.

Still, there she and I were in what we dancers call the rehearsal hall (a room in the building across from the Festival Theatre) to get our initial instructions. We started by joining hands and "circle left" and then "circle right."

I mastered that immediately.

Then we went around in a circle exchanging handshakes with alternating right and left hands until we were back in our original spot. Once again I starred.

Then it got trickier. There were moves where the

women went to the centre and the men stayed on the outside. Promenading a different woman each time, we completed a circle until we were back with our partners. Then there was an intricate (well, for us anyway) move where one couple wove in between other couples as we walked in a circle. What this has to do with goats was never explained, but it was almost 8 p.m. – showtime!

They seated us near the stage for easy access later. As the play's end neared, we heard our cue and made our way onstage as the actors were finishing their final lines. (For an instant I was just a few feet from Stratford veteran Seana McKenna – I'm sure it was a highlight of her career too).

Then it was our turn. The two actors in our group were Sanjay Talwar, who played Touchstone, and Deirdre Gillard-Rowlings, who played Audrey. The music started and we were off with our circle left and then our circle right.

I nailed it.

The rest of the dance, which lasted mere minutes, went by in a blur. I'd like to think all eyes were on me, but since we were in a group tucked upstage behind others, only select audience members probably caught all my moves. Ahh, those fortunate souls.

We seemed to get through with only minor mistakes although the weaving-of-couples part seemed a bit, umm, let's call it quirky. Still, lots of fun. The audience appeared to like it (was that standing ovation for *moi*?), and we all took our bows before heading backstage.

A few of the cast, including Petrina Bromley who played Rosalind, stopped by afterward to thank us and told us how "great" we were. I think we were only the second group of couples to perform on stage by then, so there probably hadn't been much of a bar set against which to compare us. To one of the actors, I said with tongue in cheek, "so, *this* is acting." He replied in similar fashion, "you'll take away our jobs."

No worries there for him. I've known for a long time I was never going to make it as an actor. Even my starring role as one of the "little kids" in my Grade 8 production of something called *Hippie Christmas* was never going to rocket me into the pantheon of thespian greats. And my writing has never carried me to the Festival Theatre either.

So, I'm left with my dancing. I don't know, maybe now is the time for me to chuck it all and head to Broadway or the West End. Just a kid at heart, and his dancing shoes, chasing the dream.

About the Authors

Suzanne Boles is an award-winning feature and personal essay writer with hundreds of published articles in print and online. A writing instructor at Western University Continuing Studies for over 10 years, Suzanne has helped many of her students become published writers. Visit www.suzanneboles.com for more information.

Melanie Chambers' 16 years as a travel writer to over 40 countries has produced adventure stories in markets such as Outside Magazine, Canadian Geographical, The Toronto Star, Canadian Cycling Magazine, The Globe and Mail and Mountain Life. When she's not on the road, she teaches food and travel writing courses at Western University.

Christopher Clark is a freelance writer and journalism instructor at Western University. He plays tennis and drums, but not at the same time, and is a proud father to daughter Emily. He can be found at christopherclarkwriter.com

Catherine A. Cocchio, a 24-year member of PWAC, is gradually leaving commercial markets behind to record family stories. Splitting time between residences in Alberta and Ontario, she admits the relief of meeting deadlines can't compare to arriving on time for a flight home...... wherever that may be!

Mary Ann Colihan became immersed in the narrative of her community in 2000 when she started writing profiles of local leaders and business innovations. She has reported on environmental issues for CBC.ca and CBC Radio. She has her MA in Journalism from Western University and is a writing instructor at Western Continuing Studies.

Sheila Creighton loves storytelling in this age of information and images. For 25 years, she's connected a career in communications with freelance writing and photography. With a focus on heritage, theatre, healthcare, business and nature, Sheila has written for many audiences including books, magazines, newspapers, blogs, websites and social media.

Johnny Fansher primarily writes tributes about people who touch his life and is frequently asked to deliver eulogies and to officiate celebration of life ceremonies. A pioneer in the Canadian Responsible Investment industry, catalyst for Social Innovation, enthusiastic traveller and bona fide foodie – Johnny writes about all of these passions too!

Mark Kearney, whose work has appeared in more than 80 newspapers and magazines, is an award-winning journalist, co-author of 10 books and contributor to three others. He is a lecturer in writing and journalism at Western University and has won several awards for his teaching. His website is www.mark-kearney.com

Nicole Laidler is an award-winning writer and content consultant and the owner of Spilled Ink Writing & Wordsmithing. She uses her life-long love of words to help people find their voice through feature writing, story-based copywriting, traditional and online marketing copy, and more. www.spilledink.ca

Nancy Loucks-McSloy's work has appeared in local and national magazines and newspapers for the past 16 years. Her first story was published in Macleans on 9/11. Her work has a appeared in Flare, Women's World, Canada's History, Daytripping and more, plus several books including Chicken Soup for the Soul.

Patricia Paterson is a retired educator and communications consultant. As owner of Oracle Consulting, Pat writes about travel, history, education and senior/boomer issues. Her articles have appeared in the Renaissance Magazine, CBC, the Londoner, The Beat, and the Dorchester Story Catchers' Voices project.

Otte Rozenkrantz came to Canada from Denmark at the age of 14, and has travelled most of this wonderful country since then. He is a professor of public relations and corporate communication at Fanshawe College, and lives in London, Ontario, with his wife Jackie, three rescue dogs and a cat.

Rebecca St. Pierre is a London, Ontario-based writer and photographer. She has been writing STEM-related articles, grants and reports for non-profits, newspapers, and award-winning magazines since 2008. Her work can be found at the Western University website and in the Canadian Medical Hall of Fame. For more information, visit www.WordFlightAndLight.com.

Sue Sutherland-Wood has been published in both Canada and the U.S. and has won several writing contests, most recently the Barbara Novack Prize for Excellence in Humour. Read more of Sue's writing at www.speranzanow.com.

Evelyn Symons is a writer and photographer living in London, Ontario. Her true passion is nature and with the help of her camera and pen she shares the spirits of nature whenever possible. Her website is www.evelynsymons.com

Kym Wolfe is a freelance writer and author of three previous books. She has written for dozens of magazines and newspapers about things that capture her interest: people and places, the arts, business, and travel. She grew up in Northern Ontario but now lives in London (in Canada). Visit her at www.kymwolfe.com.